Wool and Wine

People, Passion, Conversations

by John Martin

ISBN 978-0-692-98534-2

Contents

Foreword

I have been asked what the most interesting thing about putting this book together was. Without a doubt, it has been learning about all of the people who are highlighted in the book. Yes, I learned a lot about wines and yarns and the production of both and yes, it was great fun conducting the photoshoots with my daughter but I can safely say that for me the stories are the best part.

And the stories we have collected are absolutely wonderful! Several of the winemakers come from families with long histories in the industry and are proud of their legacies. Others just decided one day that they wanted to own a vineyard. Several of the dyers were taught to knit and fell in love with yarn at an early age; some turned to knitting as a form of therapy to help them through a tough time. One of our vintners was the first female winemaker in Colorado. A fiber artist started to learn to knit on orders from his doctor after he broke his arm when he was nine. Many of the wineries are passionate about environmental conservation and sustainability and incorporate that into their operations. Several people are

big fans of bees including one individual who decided to raise them in Philadelphia. It was my privilege to be able to talk with all of the individuals highlighted on these pages and have them share pieces of their lives with me and to be allowed, in turn, to share them with you.

My own story is far less interesting I am afraid. Like many of our collaborators, I was exposed to yarn and knitting by my grandmother when I was small. She kept everyone's feet warm with an endless array of slippers when I was younger and I remember her allowing us to select the yarn color we wanted from the big basket she kept next to her. I did not think about yarn again until much later when my wife began to learn how to knit. As she began filling our house with projects, I found out that there was a lot more to it than I was aware of. Speckled yarn? Self-stripping? Yak and alpaca? What happened to the red and blue cotton yarn that I remembered? Watching her work and seeing what developed was even more amazing. Hats and scarves seemed natural enough but the sweaters and lace shawls that I saw being made seemed more

like something that I would expect to have to purchase in a store. And of course, there were socks – never had I ever worn socks such as these before. In fact, because I have small feet, I do not think that I ever had socks that fit properly before my wife made me a pair – custom fit to my foot; who would have thought it was possible!

I also owe my interest in wine to my wife. For a long period, she lived in the Bay Area of California. While she eventually moved to the East Coast to be with me, her father remained in California. On our first trip back to visit him, they took me on my first wine tasting. We visited three wineries that day beginning with Dry Creek Vineyards. Being relatively young, I selected wine based on price more than anything else and a whole new world was opened up to me with that first flight. The employee was friendly and helpful and guided me through all of the correct steps of a proper evaluation. I learned that there is a lot of difference between one wine and another, from one vineyard and its neighbor, from one bottle to the next and when in doubt you usually cannot go wrong with a Pinot Noir. It was a thrill to have Dry Creek Vineyards agree to be part of this book, as I will always have fond memories of that first visit with them.

The inspiration to bring these interests together actually had nothing to do with either yarn or wine but education. I was taking a class as part of my Master's program and needed to have a "project" to develop as part of one of the courses. I did not have an actual project to work on so I needed to make one up. I had always thought that writing a book would be interesting and when I proposed the idea, the instructor was supportive. The subject of yarn and wine developed over time as something that had a lot of personal interest for me as well as something that would be of interest to my wife. The course went well and in the final comments that I received from my professor, she said that the book sounded interesting and I should let her know if I ever actually wrote it.

With that encouragement, I decided to give it a try. I started to reach out to

individuals involved in dying and winemaking; connections were made and stories started to be collected. I tried to begin my interviews by focusing on finding out some basic information such as why the participants decided to pursue this profession, how they learned their skills and what keeps them inspired and creating these amazing things. From there, we talked about a wide variety of topics as they enthusiastically told me of their individual journeys including highlights, funny stories and hopes for the future. The more I learned, the more I saw that at their core, these folks have a lot more in common than you might

anticipate. They are artisans, focused on the art of what they do and it is their creativity that really makes the products that they produce unique. They all started with a dream and worked extremely hard to make it a reality, overcoming challenges to arrive where they are today. And, perhaps most importantly, they were all bold enough to act on an idea, throw caution into the wind and risk a lot to become successful in their chosen fields. It was an amazing experience getting to know them.

I hope that you enjoy their stories.

The Pairings

Eden Cottage Yarns
McGrail Vineyards and Winery

Yarn: *Milburn 4ply; Thyme and Black Tulip*
Luxury, Unique, Soft, Rich, Complimentary

Wine: *2016 Peyton Paige Sauvignon Blanc*
Refreshing, Crisp, Tropical Fruit, Supple, Delicious

The deep, muted colors of the yarn will work well with a variety of patterns and provide a rich, classic feel to any project. The wine is bright and versatile; ideal with a range of foods from spicy to savory. Together they create a light, delicate pairing which conveys luxury and understated elegance.

Eden Cottage Yarns
Victoria Magnus

The Baxter family was the world's first and largest linen manufacturer in the mid to late 1800s and they founded the University of Dundee, in Dundee, Scotland, in 1881. While the university has grown and presently offers a wide range of courses and degrees, it has remained true to its heritage and has a particularly strong program in Art, Design & Architecture with many students focused on textile creation and design. Victoria Magnus studied Architecture there for four years, and found it a creative and stimulating place to be.

Cornhill by Victoria Magnus

Inspired by seeing textile students' work in the same building as the architecture studios, she taught herself to knit in 2006, guided by information on the internet. Her first project was a Fairisle hot water bottle cover in black and purple and while it might not have won any prizes, she was hooked from the start. From there, things spiraled out of control a bit, as she pursued spinning and then moved on to dyeing. "If you are creative minded, you are interested in trying everything," she explains with a laugh.

Years later, she decided to leave architecture, realizing it wasn't the calling for her and spent the next few years in a variety of jobs that somehow always managed to be craft or yarn related. After a drastic and unexpected life-change, she found herself moving from Manchester City Center to a crumbling 1740s farmhouse in the Eden Valley of Cumbria. She did not have any income, savings, or a job in place, but she thought that she could make a career from her yarn hobby. Moreover, if it did not work out, she was on her own

and confident that she could find a job somewhere. With little to lose, she decided to jump in with both feet and in late 2011, Eden Cottage Yarns was born.

"For as long as I can remember, I have loved to create," says Victoria. Her creative spirit was put to the test that first year in the cottage with heat available only when she could purchase coal and little income as she struggled to get her business started. Nevertheless, she made it through, fixing up the house and focusing on her fledgling business. Slowly but steadily word spread about the wonderful products and colors coming out of the cottage and eventually Victoria was able to reach a milestone – she was able to pay the bills as well as make a wage doing something that she absolutely loved.

"Say yes to opportunities"

Her enthusiasm shines through in her products and today Eden Cottage Yarns is known for their dusky, muted and vintage inspired colorways. "I take most of my inspiration from nature," says Victoria. "I like nothing more than walking my dog through the countryside snapping pictures. The most difficult part of the process is remembering where the gaps are currently in my color palette. I tend to go mostly for greens and pinks!"

One thing that people may not realize about the dyeing process is that all of Victoria's colors start as seven basic color powders. Honing the recipes to get an exact shade is a long, painstaking process and any changes to the components can have a huge impact on the final product. Today, as it was at the start, all of the yarn is dyed in her kitchen and

hung outside in the garden to dry. That is set to change soon, though with the construction of a workshop and office on her property. It has been a long time coming and she is looking forward to being able to use her kitchen as a kitchen again!

The bases that Eden Cottage utilizes for its yarns include Merino, Bluefaced Leicester, Polwarth, Alpaca and Yak with variations of yarn weight and in a number of different mixtures. "I chose these as they are my favorite yarns to work with," explains Victoria. "I have experimented with a number of different wools but they have to be up to standard for me to want to use them on a regular basis."

As a small business owner, Victoria finds a lot to love about what she does – "the fact that I have creative output, hearing positive feedback from customers, seeing finished products and getting to work from home" among them. There have been some surprising challenges along the way as well. "I was astounded by the amount of tax and overhead that small businesses actually incur - even an online one," she says. "The amount of paperwork that is required to keep track of it all is enormous."

Inspiration can also be elusive when you are working flat out and are pushing yourself to the limits. "Stress and tiredness are a major hindrance to new ideas. This is especially true in the run up to big shows, with the pressure of planning how the stall with look, working out how much yarn to take, colors and yarn types, and then getting it all dyed and labelled in time. No matter how early we start planning it never seems to be enough!"

Judging by the popularity of Eden Cottage Yarns, Victoria's many customers value her efforts and seeing people enjoying the yarns keeps her going. "I love to see Eden Cottage Yarn in the wild – with people using my yarn and patterns," she says with a smile. "I want people to use and enjoy them as much as I do!"

Fun Fact:
Victoria was a belly dancer at one time.

Looking forward, Victoria is hoping to see her business continue to grow and expand. "At the moment I am happy with where the business is at. We have a few new lines in the pipeline but I mostly want to focus on growing productivity.

I have staff now, so anything is possible!"

What does she like to do in her free time? "I don't tend to get a lot of spare time, but when I do I like reading, spending time with my dog, gardening, socializing and board games." And knitting of course, which has continued to be a passion since she taught herself in her University days. "Knitting is my way to switch off after a busy day. My Ravelry queue is HUGE. I want to knit everything and so the list keeps growing!"

"The colors of our Milburn 4ply range were directly taken from our most popular hand-dyed colorways and I am so proud of how they have come out. These shades (Thyme and Black Tulip) have been very popular so far and I love these two together. I also like that it probably wouldn't be the first combination that people might choose. It really backs up how versatile the palette is. Cornhill is one of the patterns I am most proud of. It has been very popular so far, partly because it is a good choice for beginners but also appeals to a wider audience of knitters." - Victoria

McGrail Vineyards & Winery
The McGrail Family

Heather McGrail had a dilemma on her hands. She was on the phone with her mother, Ginger, who was explaining to her that the family, who had been growing and providing grapes for winemaking in the Livermore Valley of California for a few years, had decided to take a big step and start a winery of their own. If Heather was interested, they would love for her to come home and help. Heather had left Livermore some years earlier because she was dissatisfied with a job selling wines and as she recalls, "I said I'd never work in the wine industry again." While listening to her mother explain the business plans, she received another call and clicked over to the other line – it was her father, Jim. He excitedly informed his daughter that they were going to start a winery and asked how soon she could be back.

"It's a fun way to live"

When Heather got her mother back on the line, Ginger said that she did not have to move back but that they would love to have her if she was interested. Clicking back to

Jim, she heard "get home as soon as possible." With visions of her parents sitting next to each other on two different phones trying to persuade their wayward daughter to join them in their new business, Heather wondered what she should do.

Jim and Ginger McGrail had met in high school and worked hard all of their lives to provide for their family. Ginger worked in real estate. Jim was an Alameda County deputy sheriff for 15 years; went to night school, passed the bar and became a lawyer. When a piece of hilltop property on Greenville Road became available, the couple were interested more because they liked the view than with an eye towards growing grapes. Friend Phil Wente encouraged Jim to plant the property, but at first he refused. Phil persisted and according to family lore, after one glass of wine, Jim said the idea was "crazy"; after one bottle, he "wanted Phil to tell him more"; and after perhaps one too many bottles was thinking, "that's a great idea!"

As a man who is true to his word, Jim was left with no other choice but to push forward. He had the soil tested and learned that the sandy loam was good for Cabernet Sauvignon, which

was fortunate because that was all that he liked to drink.

The McGrail's planted their Cabernet Sauvignon vineyard in 1999 and originally sold all of their fruit to the Steven Kent Winery. In those early years, they relied a lot on help and suggestions from other vineyard professionals across the Valley to learn the best ways to grow grapes and establish a high quality vineyard. In 2003, they set aside a barrel of wine to enjoy with their friends and family. It was so well received that the following vintage, one barrel turned into five and by 2005, the McGrail's were producing 1,000 cases of wine and Jim had officially caught the wine making bug.

That year also saw another event which would impact the family's fortunes. Livermore, as well as the rest of California, experienced a glut of grapes when the state produced its biggest crop ever. The McGrail's vines produced 30 extra tons of fruit, which, given the market conditions, they were not able to find a buyer for. Not ones to let anything go to waste, Jim and Ginger talked it over and said "what the heck, let's try and make our own wine". Not having their own facilities, in 2005 and 2006 they worked with other wineries in the area but in 2007 they decided to build a winery and go into production on their own.

If they were going to make it work however, they needed to get some help. Jim and Ginger's son had followed his father into law enforcement and was not able to assist with their new business. Their youngest daughter was still in college, so that left Heather as the one that they initially reached out to. That is how they came to be on the phone with her one day in early 2007 trying to convince her to return and be part of the family business. Even more important to Jim than what the business might become was the opportunity for the family to work on it together. "I don't know if I've ever really loved wine", says Jim. "I've always liked it of course, but I never thought too

much about where it came from or how it was made. This was an opportunity for our family to do something together." Whether it was Ginger, Jim, or some combination of their words, Heather decided to move home to help finish the building and open the winery. In late 2007, they brought all of their wine home and all of the blending and bottling was done at their new facility, which opened officially in April of 2008.

When McGrail Vineyards opened, it was unusual in that it only had one wine. According to Heather, "When my dad first started the winery, he said that we're going to make one bottle of wine right before we make anything else." That first wine was a Cabernet Sauvignon. While that made for some challenges for Heather in the tasting room – "it is difficult to present a nice tasting flight with just one wine" – the vineyard's hilltop location is perfect for these types of grapes with its cool evenings and early morning fog, followed by a very warm afternoon sun. The family worked with Mark Clarin, first as a consultant, then as the vineyard's full-time wine maker, to perfect their processes.

In 2012, Heather was at a wine tasting when she received a call

saying that McGrail Vineyards had won a Sweepstakes Award. She thanked the caller and politely hung up. Her phone rang again about a minute later and the same caller quickly said "I don't think that you understand what this means. This is the best red wine that we tasted. Just wait." The award was the prestigious Red Sweepstakes Award in the 2012 San Francisco Chronicle Wine competition and the winner was McGrail Vineyards' 2008 Reserve Livermore Valley Cabernet Sauvignon. That award changed everything for the young vineyard. They sold out of their Cabernet in a month and they started to think about what additional wines they could start to make.

Today, McGrail vineyards offers a number of Bordeaux varietals (merlot, red blends) which was a natural progression from their original cabernet. Winemaker Clarin's favorite varietal is a Sauvignon Blanc, which was added to compliment the reds, and they have introduced a Rosé, which much to everyone's surprise, Jim enjoys on occasion on a hot summer evening. The family also has a Chardonnay because it is Ginger's favorite wine and when you are a family business, you get to make what you want!

Along with the success of the winery, Jim's dream of making it into a family business has also become a reality. In 2009, their daughter-in-law, Rachel joined the team and Jim and Ginger's youngest daughter, Shannon came on board in 2012. Many of their wines are named after the grandchildren who happily play among the vines and Jim is already starting to work on convincing the next generation to embrace winemaking. Will he succeed? No one knows what the future may hold but for the McGrail's, winemaking has become a way of life. If everyone in the family who wants to be involved is and they can have fun doing it, they will be happy with that.

Fun Fact:
The classic 1946 Mac truck at the entrance to the Vinyard is owned by Jim McGrail

"This is the perfect summertime wine. The 2016 Peyton Paige Sauvignon Blanc is named for the first two granddaughters in the McGrail family. It has a unique creaminess and roundness on the pallet due to the use of oak barrels in its aging. The bouquet has notes of honeysuckle, white nectarine, tropical fruit and a hint of sweet basil. The flavors are a complex blend of gooseberry, honeydew melon, peaches and a hint of vanilla. It is refreshing and crisp but not as tart as some other Sauvignon Blancs." - Heather

Bartlettyarns, Inc.
Black Ankle Vineyards

Yarn: 2-Ply; Wild Grape, Raspberry, Wheat, Black and White
Historic, Natural, Warm, Long Lasting

Wine: 2014 Rolling Hills
Interesting, Complementary, Concentrated, Balanced

The unique production of the yarn gives it a historic and warm feel which is ideal for those projects requiring a timeless quality.
The wine has a very European air about it. When taken together, it is very easy to picture oneself in a warm sweater on a bright, crisp day, sitting in an outdoor cafe enjoying a glass of wine.

Bartlettyarns, Inc.
Lindsey and Susan Rice

Bartlettyarns has been processing wool alongside Higgins Stream in Harmony, Maine since its founding in 1821 by Ozias Bartlett. It utilized water power in those days and continued to operate in its original building for almost 100 years until a fire burned it to the ground in 1920. The Bartlett family began rebuilding the facility almost immediately, completing the current three-story mill building the following year, and continued to run the business until 1947. The mill has changed hands periodically in the decades that have followed but has always remained a viable business.

Susan and Lindsey Rice happened upon the mill in the early 1980s. Lindsey, a professional firefighter, raised Hampshire sheep, sheared sheep throughout New England and enjoyed demonstrating shearing at local schools on his days off. Susan knew how to sew, knit and crochet. What they needed was a place to process all of the wool that Lindsey's flock was producing, turning it into something that Susan could utilize for her projects. After some research, they decided to drive four hours

Spring in the Meadow by Bartlettyarns, Inc.

to Maine to visit Bartlettyarns in the hopes of finding a solution to their dilemma. They talked to the owners and worked out an arrangement with Susan selecting eight colors for the final yarns.

With that first batch of yarn, Susan started a knitting business called "Have Ewe Any Wool?" Over the years, the business grew and the couple made

many subsequent trips to the mill with their two children. On one trip in 1990, they turned the corner only to discover that Bartlettyarns had been transformed into a movie set – they were filming the film adaptation of Stephen King's *Graveyard Shift!* Another trip was almost for naught, as the mill's spinning mule was not working when they arrived. Lindsey, who had some experience with fixing machinery, was recruited to help and in 20 minutes it was back up and running. Lindsey was contacted a few years later when the mule was again not working and was able to perform his magic and get it going once more. On his way home, he jokingly said, "Call me if you ever want to retire and sell the business." Well, it turns out that the owner wanted to and he contacted the Rices a few weeks later to gauge their interest in buying the mill.

As much as they loved the place, it was not an easy decision. "We did have to think long and hard before

making the decision to buy" Lindsey admits. "It was right on the precipice - it would have gone out of business within a year." They decided to go ahead and purchased the mill in 2007. What they found was antique production equipment, handwritten ledgers and many outdated business systems. They brought in computers, introduced email and accounting software and developed a website with online shopping. Susan also set to work expanding their product offering – adding bases and colors she felt would attract new customers. What they chose not to update was the production equipment. In addition to the expense, the couple felt that the equipment was what made the mill and its products special.

The heart of the operation is the last commercial spinning "mule" in the United States. It is 150 feet long and operates by replicating a spinning wheel but instead of one spindle, they are able to spin 240 at a time. The motion replicates what a hand spinner would do at home. This allows them to introduce more loft and airiness into the yarn, which results in a product that is very different from modern manufactured yarn.

The overall manufacturing process also contributes to their uniqueness. Wool is delivered to the Mill in Harmony and then shipped to South Carolina where it is commercially washed. It then travels to Philadelphia, where is it dyed before returning to Maine to be made into yarn. In most commercial processes, the yarn is dyed after it is spun into yarn. The Bartlettyarns procedure results in a "heathered" or textured look to their product, although they have recently added some skein dyed yarns to the collection to compliment their traditional offering.

Most commercial yarns are also spun from combed top on large machines that pull the fiber in such a way as to produce a smooth or 'worsted spun' finish. At Bartlettyarns, they use carded fiber and the spinning mule pulls the fiber in a back and forth motion, mimicking hand spinning and resulting in 'woolen spun' yarn. The result is a fuzzier, loftier and warmer yarn.

The yarns produced at Bartlett are known for their old-fashioned woolen look and feel, which is by design. Sometimes overlooked as "scratchy", this type of yarn is sturdy and an excellent choice for making exterior garments that will last a long time, such as heavy sweaters, mittens, hats and coats.

When it was first created, Bartlettyarns served the needs of local farmers and over the years has resisted the temptation to get too big and modern. That type of community focus was what attracted Susan and Lindsey and they are committed to preserving that same way of doing business. "Keeping the fiber stream local and viable in the United States is very important," says Lindsey. "We are focused on making knitting yarn," echoes Susan. "Everything that we do goes to local yarn shops where they're working with that local hand knitter."

Black Ankle Vineyards
Susan O'Herron and Ed Boyce

It was after midnight and Sarah O'Herron was lying in the dark, unable to sleep. She and husband Ed Boyce had been enjoying their career change from business consultants to vineyard owners. They did not know a lot about the industry at the start but were confident that their research skills would keep them from blundering too badly. They had found the wine making industry to be very friendly and willing to help the newcomers with advice and guidance. Now however, they had a problem. More specifically, 4 million problems, as an infestation of Japanese beetles had descended on their vineyard.

One of Sarah and Ed's early decisions was to commit to sustainable growing and they had tried many non-pesticide methods to control the intruders

with little success. Now, Sarah was beginning to wonder if they should alter their approach somewhat in order to save their vines. Sustainability was certainly important, but was there any flexibility that would allow them to save their business? As she continued to weigh all of their options, she could almost hear the steady "crunch, crunch, crunch" as the beetles slowly and steadily ate their way across the vineyard.

Sarah and Ed had spent years appreciating good food and wine before they began to become more serious about their hobby. Why did certain wines make some foods taste better while others ruined the meal? Why were some bold and up front with their taste while others were more subtle? How were these different wines made and how was their character brought out? After what was perhaps "one taste-test too many" according to Sarah, they decided that maybe they should find out for themselves and try their hand at making the kinds of wine that they liked to drink.

In late 2000, they became serious about evaluating whether this dream was something that they should pursue. They were both

seasoned business consultants and as such, found it easy to throw themselves into researching the wine industry. They read every wine book and magazine they could get their hands on, conducted interviews and chatted with industry veterans, attended conferences and seminars and ultimately made trips to some of the great wine regions of the world including Spain, Italy and France.

Based on all of this work, they were able to make some early decisions. The first was that they were going to need a lot of help and would need to hire a consultant, which, coming from the business world, seemed natural. The next hurdle however seemed a little more daunting. If they were going to make this work, they needed to do it in Maryland near their home in Silver Springs. "The concept was a little out there," recalls Sarah. "At the time there were only about 12 wineries in the state of Maryland and there was some doubt as to whether local wine could be successful." Their inexperience may have actually been an asset. "We came at it with a different perspective. We did not have a background in wine or agriculture. In talking with folks, we found that there was

an attitude of low expectation in the industry – an acceptance that Maryland wine could only reach a certain point. We, as outsiders, did not see what the problem was. Maybe we were just too ignorant to know that any barriers existed."

"The name Black Ankle sends minds towards imagining what thousands of years of winemakers must have looked like after stomping grapes during harvest each year. It is a reminder of the generations of traditional winegrowers who have come before us and our way of expressing our appreciation for all they have taught us about how wines should be made."

In May of 2002, after over a year of driving the back roads of Maryland, Ed and Sarah took a fortunate turn and came upon a farm on Black Ankle Road that had been formerly planted with corn and alfalfa. Nestled between two hills, the land was reminiscent of one of their trips to Europe with bight sunny fields and rocky soils, and they knew that they had found the right place. They purchased

the property and set to work making it into Black Ankle Vineyards.

In the first few years, they planted their first 22 acres of grapes, cultivated the vines, learned as much as possible about how to make them yield great wine and tried to put that knowledge into practice in their vineyard. In 2006, they had their first harvest and rested the wines in barrels until they were ready for bottling two years later. The construction of their tasting room was completed in 2008 and they opened for business.

Black Ankle Vineyards is fully committed to being an estate winery producing European style wines which are dry and sweet in both red varietals (Syrah, Cabernet Sauvignon, Cabernet Franc, Merlot, Malbec, Petit Verdot and Pinot Noir) as well as white (Albarino, Chardonnay, Grüner, Veltliner, Muscat and Viognier) and is dedicated to sustainable growing practices. "Our approach has been influenced by the slow food movement as well as our concern for bio-diversity," Ed says, noting that sustainable methodology and biodynamic systems are incorporated into all aspects of their operations. Each of

their 80,000 vines is hand-tended at least eight times each season. The tasting room and winery are built from straw, clay, stone and wood that were grown or found on the farm and the winery roof is covered in sedum, a succulent used to help temperature control. Their farmhouse has a geothermal heating system and there are solar panels installed on the winery and tasting room.

While this approach makes sense environmentally, it also helps with the quality of the wine produced at the vineyard. "Many top growers support the concept of letting the grapes connect with the environment and soil naturally," explains Sarah. "This enhances the flavors which they ultimately produce." In the past, "organic" or "semi-organic" produced wine had a stigma of perhaps not tasting as good, but Ed and Sarah are showing that you can produce high quality wine in a sustainable manner. In fact, many people who know Maryland wine say that Black Ankle has raised expectations for quality and taste while helping to put the state on the wine map.

All of which was weighing heavily on Sarah's mind as she lay thinking about her beloved vineyard being slowly eaten by Japanese beetles. Being committed to sustainable agriculture did not mean allowing their business to be left in ruin. Continuing their operation would allow them to continue to talk about how wine can be made in a manner that respects both the environment as well as the product. Ultimately the couple decided that a flexible approach was more logical and they used a pesticide to handle the beetles and later on, after losing 60% of their crop to Black Rot, decided some fungicides were necessary as well.

This has not dampened their spirits, however, and they have installed electric car charging stations at Black Ankle Vineyards and continue to look for opportunities to lessen their impact on the world around them. "I think leaving a small footprint on the Earth should be something that we all naturally strive for and not something that we just use to market ourselves," says Ed firmly as he looks proudly over Black Ankle Vineyard and the paradise that he and Sarah have created.

"Rolling Hills is a corner stone of our Vineyard and tends to be one of our most popular releases for red wine lovers. This Bordeaux-style blend is my 'go to' wine. The 2014 Rolling Hills is 46% Cabernet Sauvignon, 26% Merlot, 21% Cabernet Franc and 7% Petit Verdot. It is full-bodied, lively and balanced with a lovely lingering finish." - Sarah

Wandering Wool
Northleaf Winery

Yarn: *Saranac Fingering Gradient; Midnight on the Water*
Versatile, Luxurious, Unique, Soft, Colorful

Wine: *American Chenin Blanc*
Soft, Fruity, Spicy, Floral, Honeyed

The yarn is wonderfully soft and vibrant as its color transitions across a spectrum of blue. The wine is a delightful blend of spice and fruit which caresses the palate. Together, they evoke the memory of a warm, summer evening; sitting outside a mountain cabin overlooking a quiet lake as the moon slowly rises.

Wandering Wool
Joelle Burbank

In the early 1900s, legendary Texas fiddler Luke Thomasson wrote his classic fiddle waltz "Midnight on the Water." This haunting melody captures the feeling of cowboys returning to their bunkhouse and settling in on their front porch; putting their feet up on the water trough and watching the moonlight reflect on the water. Fast-forward over 100 years and that same tune is serving as inspiration for a new colorway created by Joelle Burbank. The song and its message of long journeys, hard work and quiet contemplation of beauty could also serve as the theme for Joelle's own journey from her earliest days learning to knit, to traveling the globe pursuing her career, to her present passion as the proprietor of Wandering Wool.

A self-described "knitter, dyer, occasional spinner, terrible sewer, coffee fanatic, hiker, traveler, tinkerer and connoisseur of color," Joelle was first bitten by the knitting bug at the age of five while watching her mother knit. "I would sit on the floor and watch her, trying to figure out how she got finished sweaters out of just yarn. The whole process

seemed magical." Wanting to create some magic herself, she started learning from her mother and later took knitting classes in elementary school. "Knitting is just looping loops over other loops to make fabric," Joelle explains, "This fascinated me as a child and hundreds of projects later it still does."

As she grew older, Burbank continued knitting and found it a great portable source of entertainment and a way to release stress. She received her B.A. degree in International Relations and Affairs from American University and went on to earn her M.A. in Security Studies from Georgetown University. Following graduation, she went to work for an international development nonprofit organization and managed some of their West Africa programs. With this came a lot of travel, but she always brought her knitting. "It was a perfect way to pass the time because it was small, light, low tech and didn't need to be plugged in," she explains. And, as every knitter knows, it is a great conversation starter!

In 2011, she decided to try dyeing her own yarn for the first time. Armed with Kool-Aid at first and later with a starter

kit of commercial dyes, she found that her love of mixing and pairing different colors produced more dyed yarn than she could possibly use. "I opened a shop on Etsy and the yarn soon started to take over my house and my life and I realized it was time to devote myself to it full time." A move from Washington D.C. to the more rural area of Gaithersburg, Maryland gave her fledgling business room to grow and allowed her to indulge her other passions for gardening and backyard chickens. For a name, she drew upon all of the time traveling with her knitting and Wandering Wool was born.

"Sometimes dyeing reminds me of my college summer job as a cook – long hours, aching feet and back, a few burns here and there – and I have to laugh at the long detour through college and graduate school just to end up standing over a hot stove again!"

Joelle draws a lot of her inspiration from colors or combinations of colors that she has seen in nature and on her travels. Many of the colorways and yarn bases that she offers

Miso by Ambah O'Brien

are named after places she has visited or destinations she dreams of traveling to in the future. Her specialty is gradient yarns and she utilizes a variety of commercially sourced wool and wool blend yarns in all weights from lace to bulky. "These work great for garments when customers are looking for something that's a little easier to care for," she explains. She is also working with some yarns sourced from a local small farm and hopes to use more of these in the future. "Breed-specific yarns in particular can be a lot of fun to work with because different types of wool will give a totally different character to the yarn." She makes all of

her own blanks so that she can use any length or yarn base she likes rather than relying on commercially available sock blanks, allowing her to offer her gradient yarns in combinations of bases and yardages not found anywhere else.

While she often starts with an idea in mind of the colorway she wants to create, Joelle enjoys the process when there is no rigid guidance on how it needs to turn out. "I like to allow the colors to evolve into something new and surprise me," she says. In fact, many times she has started with one vision in her mind only to end up with something quite different.

"That happens often - maybe more often than not - and that's the fun of all this! Many of my most popular colorways started out as 'mistakes'."

Reflecting on the growth of Wandering Wool, Joelle admits that the fun part of making beautiful yarn is creating new colorways. The less glamorous, but still vital activities of keeping the books, paying the bills, shipping orders, marketing and attending festivals can be challenging. "There are times of the year that are particularly busy, especially the fall show season, and it can be hard to remain creatively inspired when working on that kind of production schedule," she explains. "I know that these things go in cycles and that when things slow down again, I can take time to explore new products and colors and rejuvenate my creativity. What's also important for me to stay inspired is making sure I give myself time to knit things just for fun."

When asked about the future, Ms. Burbank is full of energy and enthusiasm. Professionally, she would like to focus more on gradient yarns and starting to offer those in a wider range of colors, sizes and yarn bases, including more yarns sourced from local farms. She has started painting silk scarves and would like to add that to her repertoire. Natural dyes are also something she has always wanted to experiment with.

When not busy in her studio, what activities claim her attention? "I do a lot of other fiber arts including crochet, weaving, spinning and sewing," she says, quickly ticking off a list. "I would like to learn how to weld in order to make things from metal. I also love gardening and I grow vegetables and raise chickens in my backyard. I enjoy outdoor activities like hiking and camping and I play the viola."

When playing her viola, she often plays fiddle music. That allowed her to discover Luke Thomasson and "Midnight on the Water" which served as the inspiration for one of her favorite colorways. And just as the cowboys who inspired the song, it is easy to picture Joelle Burbank returning from one of her wandering trips, sitting down to enjoy the quiet and contemplating the moon reflecting on the water.

Northleaf Winery
Gail and John Nordlof

There is no specific count of how many home winemakers there are but a number of different estimates place the number at approximately one million in the United States and Canada. In most cases, these hobbyists enjoy making their own vintages to share with friends and family and they never grow beyond that. In some rare instances, the hobby continues to expand until eventually the hobby becomes a business. Such is the case with Gail and John Nordlof of Northleaf Winery in Milton, Wisconsin.

Gail's father and grandfather both made wine and although she did not learn the process from them, they may have had something to do with her starting to drink wine at the age of two! That early experience was the start of a lifelong interest and passion. "It's an amazing, living thing. It evolves. If you open a bottle of the same wine today and next year, they are a completely different thing. How can that not fascinate you," explains Gail.

While her professional path included 30 years as a software designer and consultant, she remained an avid wine fan – an interest shared with her husband, John. In fact, it was John who stoked Gail's interest in making her own wine. He was making beer at home and built himself a brewing room in their garage. That got her to thinking, "If he can make beer, I can certainly make wine!" So, she claimed a small part of the brew room and it was not too long before there was more wine equipment in there than brewing equipment. "Just like our closet, my stuff took up all the room and he got a little corner," explains Gail with a laugh. "He says he had to build me a winery to get me out of his brew room!"

When asked to describe winemaking in five words, Gail replied, "Quality time with my husband!"

Gail honed her skills through trial and error. She spoke with other home winemakers, did her own research and refined her processes. "I don't think that I have a particularly gifted palate, but I have developed the ability to distinguish what a wine made from some specific grape should taste like and to recognize the layers of complex flavors in a wine that are characteristic of the different types of grapes. It's a learned skill, one you can develop if you take the time to smell and taste and think about those scents and flavors." Her first batch of amateur wine was a Barolo and when she was comfortable enough to declare herself a professional wine maker in 2008, she produced an Alsatian Gewurztraminer.

When they thought of potentially going commercial, Gail ramped up the size of her batches from 5 gallons to 25 gallons to make sure that everything worked the same way. With their garage already bursting at the seams, they needed a new location for the operation. The solution came in the form of an 1850 wheat warehouse that was on the National Register of Historic Places. The building, and a number of others nearby, are unlike any others in the United States. They are made of indigenous materials using a "mortar grout" technique. The grout itself is made from limestone aggregate dug locally and mixed with sand and water and poured into forms one foot thick. The result is a construction which can stand the test of time and this particular building had lived a long life as first the wheat warehouse and then a garage and machine shop (catering to both automobiles and carriages) followed by a car dealership to finally becoming the Sunnyview Apple Orchard Warehouse until that business closed in 1991. The local historical society took possession and it was from them that the Nordlof's purchased the property.

Gail was charmed by the quaintness of the triple doors in front and the barn-sash windows and immediately thought "this would make a

perfect winery". John's first thought was "this is going to cost our life savings!" They begin their restoration in 2007, situating their tasting room in the warehouse and adding a wine cellar, bottling area and warehouse to the back. They opened their doors for business in 2009.

Almost immediately, they faced a significant challenge. The year 2009 in the United States brought with it a recession but "there was no going back" Gail recalls. Making batches ten times bigger than what she had made at home also presented some difficulties, not the least of which was that they were using mostly Italian equipment and the instructions were all in Italian (which she didn't speak)! However, working together with her husband and family, they were able to make Northleaf Winery a success. Today the family-run business has three generations involved in crafting about 25 wines in small batches at any given time.

Gail uses the classic grape varietals for the most part; "the varietals everyone knows, or at least has heard of, so they can name something they know and we have it or something like it." They are sourced from coast to coast as well as in their

local Wisconsin. "I experiment with blending different varietals and blending different fruits and fruit flavors (green apple, peach, pineapple/mango, pomegranate, cranberry, raspberry) with varietals" and solicit both their customers and wine club for feedback to help dictate future direction.

Gail utilizes a very traditional winemaking method in order to ensure the consistency of her product. This approach generally has a predicable result, but there was one time where she ended up with a surprise at the end. "I normally guide the process we use to make port; however I did once allow my husband and a friend of ours to blend it. It turned out to be particularly potent!" While not confirmed, that may have been the last time that John was allowed to take the reins in the winery.

Being a very small winery, the family does everything.

"We're the tour guides, the marketers, the bookkeepers, the secretary, human resources, the computer engineers, the legal department, the gardeners, the copywriters, the handymen, AND the janitors" say Gail. On bottling day their kids, grandkids, friends and family come together to staff the bottling line but looking ahead, she would not change a thing. "We want to remain a small, family winery. We had a very modest goal when we started the winery and have met with more success than we would have imaged. We are very grateful to our customers for all the support they give us."

They are a TravelGreen Wisconsin company and as such are always looking for ways to save resources, restore, recycle and reuse, which can lead to some innovations; for example, they just switched from real cork to zero-carbon footprint corks made out of sugar cane. They also have plans to create a tap-room next door - it would be such a complimentary business and "the two would have so much synergy together!" John may not have taken his home brewing hobby to a completely new level yet, but he could certainly support other brewers who have.

"Chenin Blanc has been an underestimated varietal for a very long time. It is now having a kind of renaissance around the world - it's a great value and can be successfully made into a wide array of styles. Our Chenin Blanc is just off-dry, with a hint of sweet, almost unnoticeable. It has a zesty, fruit and honey quality, almost spicey, and plenty of refreshing acidity." - Gail

Rosy Green Wool
Pedroncelli Winery

Yarn: *Cheeky Merino Joy; Blackberry, Sand*
Organic, Soft, Vibrant, Sustainable, Cozy

Wine: *2015 Mother Clone Dry Creek Valley Zinfandel*
Spices, Fruit, Smooth, Friendly, Versatile

In complimentary shades, the sustainably produced yarn has deep color and a luxurious quality which would benefit any pattern. The wine has a spice to it which does not overpower and provides a hint of fruit which lingers on the palate. This pairing is like old friends getting together for a night of reminisincing by the fire - warm and friendly with plenty of laughter and smiles.

Rosy Green Wool
Rosy Stegmann / Patrick Grubaen

Where does your yarn come from? How does it make its way from the sheep to your door? Many of us take the process for granted but Rosy Stegmann wanted to ensure that she was aware of what the yarn she was using went through at every step in the process. Rosy and her partner, Patrick Grubaen, had preferred organic food for a long time and since she was a frequent and passionate knitter, it was only natural that she wanted to find organic wool. This quest started them on a path that culminated in the creation of their own company, Rosy Green Wool.

As Rosy started her research she began to discover many things that alarmed her from the painful mulesing that Merino sheep suffer to the large quantities of chemicals and pesticides that are normally used in yarn production. What she was not able to find was an organic wool that offered a verifiable guarantee that its production did not harm the sheep or environment while at the same time being soft and available undyed. Frustrated, Rosy was faced a big challenge. "It was simply

impossible for me to continue knitting with such yarns and feeling good at the same time," she explains.

The most comprehensive international transparency and guarantee of organic production that the two were able to find was that of the Global Organic Textile Standard (GOTS). But how could they obtain yarn produced to GOTS standards? The first important step was to find a source of extra soft Merino wool – a big hurdle because this type of wool is normally only shipped in batches of 20 tons or more from South America, New Zealand and Australia. The next step would be to find a spinning mill and a dyer who were certifiably organic as well.

Overcoming the challenges of obtaining and providing organic wool and yarn would have been daunting on an individual level, so Rosy and Patrick founded Rosy Green Wool together in 2012. For their spinning and dying needs, they needed to locate GOTS certified facilities that were able to work with the smaller batches of wool that their start-up company would be purchasing. They were able to find those in England, with its long tradition of spinning, dyeing and weaving. "We

liked the concept of working closely together with small businesses where many things are still done manually and who share our love of nature, sheep and wool," explains Rosy. "It was, and is, important for us to work together with our partners to achieve the special quality of our yarn." That type of production environment is something that she was well versed in because grandparents had founded a small spinning mill in Southern Germany in the 1950s which was later passed on to her parents. "As I child, I grew up with the smell of wool and of course there was a lot of knitting and crocheting happening in my family."

Patrick and Rosy had created a company and found a solution for obtaining organic yarn, but they wanted to offer more than just nice words on their website. They decided to become GOTS certified themselves, a big commitment for a small company. "We want to help reduce cruelty to animals, make the work place better for workers in the textile industry and provide customers a sustainable choice for yarn," they explain. Working closely with their small spinning mill and dye house, Rosy created the first two offerings for Rosy Green Wool, two 100% organic Merino yarns in 16 colors: Cheeky Merino Joy and Big Merino Hug.

Organic area

Like many others just starting a business, the two often struggled to find the time for their business while they were both working other jobs. There were times when they asked themselves how many evenings and weekends they could work without compromising their health. Luckily, as their business started to grow, they were able to adjust their schedules to support the business and

Rosy started to focus on it full time in 2013. One of their early supporters was designer Melanie Berg. She approached Rosy and Patrick while they were still not well known about designing a pattern for their organic yarn. The result was Drachenfels, which became one of the 20 most popular patterns on Ravelry, bringing Rosy Green Wool important visibility and starting a collaboration that has resulted in many more patterns, as well as a friendship.

Looking to further expand their business and enter into the United States market, Rosy and Patrick journeyed to New York City for the holidays in 2013. They had reached out to a distributor in Long Island and were excited to be invited to visit. Taking the train from New York, they were picked up at the station by a company employee and settled in a meeting room where they prepared for their presentation. A few moments later, the CEO entered to start the meeting. He picked up the yarn that had been laid out on the table and immediately said, "This is not going to work". Within seconds he had determined that the yarn that Rosy had worked so hard to find and develop would be too expensive to sell.

Luckily, the two were determined to succeed and continued to make and promote their yarns and the benefits of organic production. Help came from their friend Melanie Berg who introduced them to an alternative distributor a year later and Rosy Green Wool became more widely available in North America. That year, 2014, was memorable for another reason as well – Patrick and Rosy were married and happily created a husband and wife team determined to continue to improve the world around them.

Despite the restrictions that come along with GOTS certified dyeing, Rosy continues to work closely with their dye house to expand the colors that Rosy Green Wool offers. "We look at nature and work with various textile color samples to find interesting combinations, harmonies and contrasts. This usually results in many interesting options from which we can pick only a few for the next one or two seasons." They have also recently begun to process wool from sheep breeds that are rare and in danger of extinction. Patrick says that they "would love to get fibres from other animals but organic production is still very rare."

While still just a two-person company operating from their small flat in Munich, Rosy and Patrick are having a big impact. A share of their revenue of rare breed yarn goes to support the Rare Breeds Survival Trust. They are also excited that after five years of being one of only a small handful of GOTS certified yarn providers, they are now seeing some others choosing to pursue that certification as well. And after the hectic pace of their early years in business together, they are now often able to take a few extra days while visiting their supplier in the UK – walking the countryside together, enjoying the views of the landscape and the sheep which they care so much about protecting.

Faberge by Laura Aylor

32

Pedroncelli Winery
Pedroncelli Family / Montse Reece

January 17, 1920 marked a momentous point in the history of the United States. On that day, the 18th Amendment to the US Constitution became law and the country officially became "dry" – the sale of alcohol was illegal. It was with great vision that Giovanni and Julia Pedroncelli purchased a vineyard, shuttered winery and home in Sonoma County, California a few years later. While many vineyards went out of business and other purveyors of "Demon Rum" continued to ply their trade on the sly, the Pedroncelli's sold grapes to home winemakers during the prohibition years to keep their vineyard going and family supported. On March 22, 1933, President Roosevelt signed the Cullen-Harrison Act legalizing the sale of beer and wine. Before the end of the year the 25th Amendment to the Constitution was passed, repealing the 18th Amendment

"Wine is like a genie trapped in the bottle. You take the cork out and release the magic!" - Polo Cano, Cellar Master

and making the sale of alcohol legal.

With happy days here once again, the Pedroncelli's applied for licensing to begin wine production. The 1934 harvest marked the start of a successful family business known for exceptional wine and innovation. John Pedroncelli Jr. became the winemaker in 1948, making him the second generation of the family to serve in that role. His brother, Jim Pedroncelli, assumed sales and marketing responsibilities in 1957 and together the two expanded the winery significantly - eventually purchasing it from their father in 1963. Among the earliest entrants into the Sonoma County wine scene, Pedroncelli winery is credited with being the first to invite consumers in to taste wines, the first to provide a Rosé made from Zinfandel, the first to plant Cabernet Sauvignon and the first to create an independent sales and marketing network.

In 2007, a young Spanish winemaker named Montse Reece joined this family wine dynasty. A native of Catalonia, Spain, she had attended Rovira I Virgili University and graduated with a degree in Agricultural Engineering and

Enology. Growing up in a culture were wine is considered a food and has deep cultural roots, Montse felt immediately at home with the Pedroncelli's and their flagship Zinfandel wine. In fact, the 2007 vintage remains her favorite vintage to date. "The 2007 vintage was the perfect vintage for zinfandel in the Dry Creek Valley," she explains. "I felt like I went back to my roots."

She worked for seven years alongside legendary vintner John Pedroncelli who by that time had produced 60 vintages. Excited by the opportunity, Montse quickly settled into her new role and became like one of the family. In 2015, however, she and the Pedroncelli family would be tested. There was a drought in Northern California that year and they had very little rain during the growing season. This stressed the vines to the point where they were harvested in August for the first time in memory. The family also experienced a loss with the passing of family patriarch John Pedroncelli.

Into this void stepped Montse, who was named winemaker later that year becoming just the third winemaker in the 90-year history of the vineyard and the first woman. Her background in Spain and time working with John before his passing made her an ideal fit. Her goal was, and still is, to "continue the style the Pedroncelli family has been making for decades. It is an old world approach to making wine were the focus is on lower alcohol, bright acidity and highlighting a variety of flavors with minimal oak treatment."

This was not the first challenging time in Ms. Reece's career. "My first harvest was in 1993 in a little cooperative in the Penedes, next to Barcelona. I thought I was going there just to help in the cellar but to my surprise, they told me I was going to be the winemaker. In the lab, there was only a dial up phone on the wall, which had taped to it the phone number of a winemaker working miles away in case I needed advice. I spent countless hours that harvest on that phone!"

Nevertheless, she succeeded and that perseverance, confidence and determination would serve her in good stead as she continued to advance her career and eventually relocate to California.

She considers winemaking a creative science and offers some practical advice to those interested in pursuing it as a career. First, find your palate – "try as many wines and wine styles as possible to find the wine that suits your own taste and story." Second, winemaking is a biological process with many different elements – "know them all." Finally, winemaking starts in the vineyard – "know your vines and how to work with them." Moreover, even with years of experience, know that there are still things that can reach out and surprise you. "In 2012, we made for the first time wine out of one small lot of Cabernet Sauvignon we grow in the Dry Creek Valley. The reason was I saw harvest after harvest how the grapes from that lot delivered a very unique wine

that always was blended into our main Cabernet Sauvignon. In 2012, we bottled for the first time this Cabernet without blending and called it Wisdom. Because the vines were much younger than all the rest, I expected it to be a quite tannic but it was a beautifully intense wine. To my surprise after aging in barrels for 18 months the tannins smoothed out so well it didn't need fining. That is quite unusual for a Cabernet Sauvignon."

With all of the challenges she has faced, Montse has never thought about being anything other than what she is – a winemaker. "At the end of the day all I want is to create an approachable but unique wine to grace the dinner table and make life a little better for whomever may be enjoying it," she says.

It would seem as if the Pedroncelli family feels much the same way. They are now into their third generation of family ownership (70% women owned) with the fourth generation firmly involved in the business as well and remain firmly committed to preserving their legacy of family and fine wines for the enjoyment of generations to come.

"2015 was a difficult vintage. It was a year of drought here in North California. We didn't have any rain during the growing season and the vines were very stressed. Zinfandel was picked for the first time in August. The wine has a high concentration of flavors due to the lack of water inside the berries. It has aromas of ripe berries mingled with hints of black pepper, cinnamon and toasty oak. Rich flavors of blackberry, plums, mocha, vanilla and dark chocolate." - Montse

Baa Baa Brighouse
Elk Cove Vineyard

Yarn: Baa Baa Brew DK; Wellholme, Bailiff Bridge
   British, Beautiful, Soft, Smooth, Rich

Wine: 2016 Pinot Noir Rosé
   Ripe, Fresh, Strawberry, Intense, Gulp-Able

Laughter and smiles - you can't help but think of those things when you handle these bright, cheerful yarns. Similarly, while enjoying the rich color and fresh taste of the wine, you find yourself thinking about spending time with loved ones. Together, they conjure up an image of a fun, family picnic - children laughing among a sunny field of wildflowers while adults tell stories on blankets in the shade.

Baa Baa Brighouse
Elaine Jinks-Turner

A survey of more than 3,500 knitters worldwide found that 81.5 percent of the respondents indicated that they felt happier after knitting. This may not seem like a revelation to those who enjoy knitting and crafting but in many cases the positive impacts go beyond the simple enjoyment of a creative hobby. There are many, many stories from individuals who have experienced a significant health benefit from knitting and credit it with having a positive impact on their lives.

Dr. Herbert Bensen, a pioneer in mind/body medicine and founder of the Mind/Body Medical Institute at Massachusetts General Hospital in Boston, has said that the repetitive action of moving needles can produce a relaxed mental state like that associated with yoga and meditation. (Repetitive movement having a powerful calming effect is also demonstrated when rocking a baby to sleep or relaxing in a rocking chair.)

Once you get beyond the initial learning curve and any frustration associated with it, knitting and crocheting have been shown to lower heart rate and blood pressure as well as reducing levels of stress producing cortisol in the blood. Craft activities also result in tangible products that can enhance self-esteem. Other health benefits that have been proven include helping smokers kick the habit, coping with crises, enhancing social skills, helping to control weight, helping with arthritis, and improving finger dexterity. Those who find these claims doubtful only have to spend a few minutes with Elaine Jinks-Turner to see the results for themselves.

Elaine has experienced mental health challenges off and on for a good portion of her adult life with major life changes such as a difficult relationship or a long distance move acting as a trigger. At first, she would cope by throwing herself into her work as a journalist but that became difficult as her family started to grow. Following the birth of her daughter Florence in 2010 and second son Benjamin in 2011, she was forced to cope with post-natal depression using new tools. She first worked with her physician to locate a medication that could provide relief but only had mixed results. Eventually, she turned to knitting, something that her mother had taught her as a child but that she had not done in quite some time.

Knitting was a tremendous help to Elaine and while she still has struggles from time to time, they are much less frequent and much more manageable. The benefits she has realized prompted her to form a regular Knit and Natter group, which has helped others cope with their own challenges. From the creation of the group and advising her friends on their yarn choices and patterns, it was just a small step to the formation of Baa Baa Brighouse in 2014.

Fulfilling Elaine's vision, Baa Baa Brighouse specializes in British and in particular, Yorkshire, yarns that have been reared, sheared, spun and dyed locally. Shortly after setting up the company, she began working with a group of Yorkshire based independent dyers on a monthly subscription club called the Yan Tan Tethera

Yarn Club. "I found their work really inspirational and as a result, Baa Baa Brew DK was the first yarn out of my own dye pot," she explains. "I wanted to create a collection that was quintessentially Yorkshire so the yarn was sourced and spun in Yorkshire, dyed by hand here using traditional small scale methods and each colorway in the collection is named after an area of Brighouse, the town in which it is produced."

For her bases, Elaine uses a British Bluefaced Leicester DK yarn and a 4 Ply 75% British Bluefaced Leicester/25% Masham yarn base. "I think as a British yarn retailer and dyer, based in Yorkshire, which is widely known for its textile heritage, it is important for me to use and promote traditional British breeds." Since local sheep provide some of the best fleeces in the world and they have access to local spinning mills, it makes perfect sense to work collaboratively as a community to enhance their shared industry.

"Color, textures, fiber. Knitting is very tactile and visual - it's like a feast for the senses!"

Jinks-Turner draws inspiration from the world around her – the landscape, nature, her own town – but often starts out with an idea in her mind of what she wants to create. She runs a monthly themed yarn subscription box that highlights popular culture and she often creates products based on a particular subject – Sherlock Holmes, Jane Austen, Beauty and the Beast or Les Miserables for example. The result is that there is usually a backstory for the colorways that are offered by Baa Baa Brighouse. Recently, Elaine introduced Baa Baa Brew Marble 4 Ply, which was inspired by an international women's march. "The collection is called 'The Mulier Fortis Collection', meaning 'strong woman' in Latin and each colorway is named after an inspirational woman who has contributed to medicine, science, education, etc."

When not tending to her growing business, Elaine keeps quite busy with her family and enjoys spending time with husband Gary and their three children, Jonathan, Florence and Benjamin, as well as exploring the countryside with their dog Meg. She also finds time to give back to her local community such as participating in a recent knitting project

with her Knit and Natter group to produce bookmarks to yarn bomb their local library with as part of National Libraries Week. Professionally, she looks forward to one day having her own brick and mortar shop. "We are just on-line at the moment but the number of people that come knocking on my front door looking for an actual shop is incredible" she says with a laugh.

Fun Fact:
Elaine can play the drums and used to sing in a band.

Reflecting back on how she arrived at where she is today, Elaine says, "If you had asked me 10 years ago, is this what I would be doing with my life, I would have laughed at you. I only ever wanted to be a journalist for as long as I can remember but hindsight is a wonderful thing. Looking back, although I enjoyed what I did, I still drew a distinction between life and work. So, was I really happy as a journalist? Probably not. With Baa Baa Brighouse, I no longer have that distinction. It is work, yes, but it is also life and I love it!"

"Bailiff Bridge and Wellholme were colors that were added to the collection in the autumn of 2016. Personally, Autumn is one of my favorite times of year. I love the vibrant, rich colors that nature throws at us and I think these two yarns are a wonderful reflection of that." - Elaine

Great Divide Shawl by Michele Brown

Elk Cove Vineyard
Campbell Family / Adam Campbell

As the Campbell family drove up a winding gravel road in Northwest Oregon, father, Joe and mother, Pat looked at the land around them. With its shallow soils, steep hilly terrain and beautiful views, the area had been a homestead at one time but was now abandoned and overgrown with prune and hazelnut trees. The property, in the foothills of the Coast Range Mountains, was just what they were looking for as the family started on a new adventure. Their six-year-old daughter, perhaps being a bit more practical, sized up the situation and asked, "Where are we going to live?" Joe and Pat smiled and happily replied, "The house is behind us!" They were pointing to the trailer that would be home for the next year. The year was 1974, and the Campbell's were about to become Oregon winegrowing pioneers.

Pat and Joe met when they were both teenagers picking strawberries for spending money. He was a small town kid from Hood River, Oregon who would go to Harvard and then Stanford Medical School. Pat's great-grandfather was

a Swiss immigrant who came to Helvetia, Oregon, grew grapes and made wine prior to prohibition. Her parents were orchardists in Parkdale, a small farming community at the foot of Mount Hood. Her father Lew, upon seeing his daughter's new land, commented, "With this soil and no water, I don't think you can grow anything here – except maybe wine grapes."

That was the plan of course. Joe used his academic background to teach himself the science of winemaking and the family set to work. The first project was converting the existing homesteader's barn into a winery, followed quickly by a second project to build a new home from reclaimed lumber to provide the family with a bit more room. That winter, a herd of 40 Roosevelt Elk bedded down in the clearing beside the Campbell family's trailer. Their presence, along with the protective bowl shape of the property, inspired Pat and Joe to name their property Elk Cove

Vineyards. At the time, there were fewer than ten wineries in Oregon.

With a lot of hard work, Elk Cove Vineyards slowly started producing. In 1979, the Campbell's 1978 Riesling won gold at the Oregon State fair, the Tri-Cities Wine Festival and the Seattle Enological Society annual tasting. Joe and Pat had shown that they could make world-class wine. Several years later, the Oregon wine industry exploded and currently there are over 500 wineries in the state. Elk Cove has grown as well and today it is made up of six vineyard sites with 350 planted acres – 10 times the total acreage of all Oregon vineyards when Pat and Joe planted those first vines.

The Campbell's son Adam is now the owner and head winemaker at the estate. Like all of Joe and Pat's kids, he spent his summers in the vineyard and on the bottling line helping with the family business. He attended Lewis & Clark College in Portland, earning a degree in political science, and then moved to Australia where he fell in love and was married. He returned to the vineyard in 1995 and joined with his parents to create Elk Cove's wine and in 1999, he become the head winemaker. Little did he know that he was jumping in at a very challenging time.

Oregon experienced a cool and wet spring in 1999, a condition that did not ease as summer came. As Adam recalls, "based on ripening data, I knew we wouldn't be picking Pinot Noir until late October and frankly that spelled disaster." So he headed into his first solo vintage facing what was possibly the worst case scenario. However, fall brought with it a change in weather and the break that Campbell needed. "We miraculously had a cool but sunny October with shockingly little rain. We picked well into mid-November under clear skies. The wines from this vintage are some of the finest ever produced in Oregon!"

The Willamette Valley is in the Yamhill-Carlton American Viticulture Area (AVA) and 80% of plantings in the valley are Pinot Noir. With soils composed mostly of marine sediments – sandy and well drained – and a cool, wet climate, the growing conditions are ideal. "Pinot Noir is the Holy grail for all of us here in this region and that is the wine that inspired my parents to plant here and what brought me home to join them," says Adam. Elk Cove today produces a variety of cool climate grapes including Pinot Noir, Pinot Gris, Pinot Blanc, Chardonnay and Riesling. According to Adam, "growing grapes in the coolest possible climate where you can still reliably ripen them is the key to getting full flavor development, complexity and freshness of fruit."

The Campbell's goal has always been handcrafted, estate grown cool climate wines that rival the best in the world. As a second-generation winemaker and a fifth generation Oregon farmer, Adam is proud to continue that tradition. "When I was growing up, my parents were pouring their heart and soul into growing grapes and making wine. They were obsessed to the point where they literally talked about wine and vineyards non-stop. At the dinner table nearly every night, my siblings and I would complain and ask them to 'quit talking about wine!'" That drive and passion somehow became ingrained in their son who loves that he is able to continue his family's farming legacy by making a value added agricultural crop that brings joy to people's lives.

Looking forward, he hopes to continue to grow the winery organically by planting new vineyards and continuing to explore new territory for viticulture. Challenges such as new microclimates, soils and higher elevations are already in his mind. Thinking back to the family who first drove up the gravel lane to start a winery in the hills, does Adam think that there will be a new generation to continue the legacy? "If I am lucky enough to have my kids get bitten by the wine bug, I would love the challenge of guiding them on a path in this amazing industry. It does not have to be winemaking and it does not have to be here at Elk Cove. I would never push them into it but I would be lying if I didn't admit that it would be an honor to have them choose this life."

And for those lucky enough to visit Elk Cove Vineyards and share some time with the Campbell's, keep your eyes open - the same herd of Roosevelt Elk who greeted the Campbell's so many years ago is still around.

"Dry, food friendly Rosé wines have been gaining in popularity. Pinot Noir is an amazing varietal for this style of wine as it has the super bright red cherry/strawberry fruit and is the best summer wine imaginable. The 2016 Pinot Noir Rosé is fun and serious at the same time. It has a nose of sweet cherry, early season strawberries and honeydew melon. A juicy palate follows with notes of tart cherry accented by rose petals and a grippy and zippy finish of lime-peel and Bosc pear." - Adam

Pik Ka Handbag
Colorado Cellars

Yarn: *Dornfelder Wine*
Marriage of Yarn and Design

Wine: *2015 Alpenglo Riesling*
Clean, Crisp, Lush, Apple, Rich

This yarn and the patterns are reflective of the scenic Montana environment in which they were made - simple, yet complex; rugged and beautiful. The wine is a nice Riesling; semi-sweet with an intense floral nose reminiscent of the great outdoors. Combined together, they bring to mind big skies, wild landscapes and thrilling adventures.

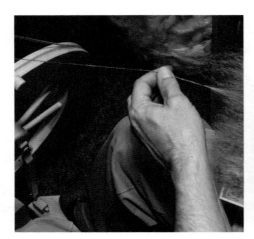

Pik Ka Handbag
Randy Glick

Randy Glick came to knitting by way of gymnastics. Nine-year old Randy was performing a handstand in gymnastics class when a friend began a tumbling run, which unfortunately ended in the exact spot Randy was occupying. When the boys untangled themselves, Randy was left with both bones in his left forearm broken and the old country doctor that set his arm recommended to his mother that taking up knitting would be great physical therapy. The prescribed treatment was followed and Randy never had any problems with his arm after the bones healed.

While both his grandmother and mother were knitters, Glick was already a member of the 4-H club in his small Wisconsin community and discovered that they offered knitting classes, which he was soon taking. "My earliest memories of knitting are in Mrs. Olefield's front yard,

"It's not the time put into the final piece the customer is buying - or the materials. It is the journey the artist took to get there... and that is priceless!"

white Red Heart Yarn and clean hands," recalls Randy. "Mrs. Olefield insisted we all use white yarn, so we were forced to wash our hands before we started each lesson. Living in a farming community, and being a boy, clean hands were never a priority and my projects sometimes showed that!"

What were those first projects? The 4-H knitting book dictated which projects the kids could do and in those days, knitting was viewed as something done mainly by young female members so the projects reflected that. "Our first project was slippers," says Randy. "You knitted a square, pulled the toe tight to draw it together and sewed up the heel. They were finished off with a pom-pom." Their first "real" project was a dress for a Barbie doll. "The reason I remember that project is because it was my first entry in the county fair. Some of the other mothers felt that it wasn't fair to have a boy competing in the knitting category with the girls."

Fast forward to the present day and Randy now calls Montana home after spending much of his adult life exploring the world in the United States Air Force. His daughter Monica, herself a fiber artist, kindled

his interest in expanding his fiber arts career to include spinning and weaving. With a process engineering background, fiber arts might not seem like a logical next step but Randy enjoys the challenge of blending his educational background with the fiber arts, taking the techniques of spinning, weaving and knitting and exploring ways to modify and perfect the methods. Along the way, he has developed improved approaches to many techniques, most notably spinning beaded yarns. His fiber art is displayed across the country and he operates Pik Ka Handbag, which specializes in one of a kind fiber creations.

"I draw my inspiration from my surroundings", explains Randy. "Here in Montana there are a lot of sheep operations both large and small. Sometimes I will take a walk on one of my friend's ranches and take reference photos that I bring into my dye studio and recreate." Most of his early work was with naturally colored wool because it was appealing to him in its original state but a close friend and mentor has a line of dyes so it was only natural that he would try his hand at dyeing as well. "My signature colors are purple, blue and cyan. I have used painted skeins and fiber in these colors for many of my knitting, weaving and felting projects."

One of Randy's biggest successes as a dyer was a project he proposed as part of his Creative Arts Enterprise degree program at Montana State University. "I proposed a project to dye over three natural colored wools with the primary colors, then plying all the various shades together. It was my most enjoyable dye project because I love the results you can get by dyeing over colored wool and the depth you get when plying them together."

For his bases, Randy likes to utilize yarns made from local wool and created in the United States. "The main reason for this is because if we don't buy local, we will end up not having local sources – whether that is wool or food." He takes a very hands-on approach in sourcing the products and has been working for several years with a local wool producer and local wool mill to create a high quality, locally sourced yarn – Smith River Targhee. For him, this provides a connection to the fiber itself. "The yarn is not what I call 'boat yarn', manufactured in some far off place. It comes from animals I have met, raised by hardworking local ranchers and processed by people I call friends."

This connection from Randy to the fiber is something that he likes to try to carry through to his designs as well. "Whether it is my felted mittens created from locally sourced Shetland sheep wool or my Chevron scarf pattern that mimics the lines of the rugged mountains surrounding the Great Falls, they all endeavor to capture some sense of the place."

Randy's past can sometimes slip into his work as well. "My grandmother, Lydia Melvin, was a knitter. There was no Walmart back then and if you had mittens, it was because someone made them for you. My grandmother had 26 grandchildren and her yearlong project was to knit each a pair of mittens for Christmas." Later in life, Randy designed a felted mitten pattern that uses Shetland sheep wool from a ranch in Montana. He called the pattern, 'Lydia's Mittens' to honor his grandmother and the love she put into her gifts every holiday.

Connections define Randy Glick. Connections to his past. Connections to the products he works with. Connections to the world around him. Whether he is designing, creating or teaching, he never loses sight of the what is important to him. As he explains, "For me art is less about making a living and more ABOUT living. It defines who I am."

Strike Up the Bands by Randy Glick

"This combination of yarn and design represents what I have become known for - yarn 'with a story' and simplicity of design. The yarn is from locally sourced wool from a beautiful ranch along the banks of the famous Smith River in north-central Montana. I have helped shear the sheep and visited/worked at the wool mill that created the final yarn. The color scheme was developed in Germany when a friend asked me to create something for his wife. When I asked what color, he simply stated 'the color of Dornfelder wine'. This design received an award at the Montana State Fair for 'Design of Enduring Quality.' " - Randy

Colorado Cellars
Rick and Padte Turley

Grapes have been grown and wine has been made in Colorado since the early 1860s when settlers brought European stocks to plant small vineyards near Penrose and Canon City. By 1882, vineyards had sprung up in Paonia, Hotchiss and Vineland and in 1890, Governor George Crawford planted 60 acres near the Town of Palisade in what is today the Grand Valley American Viticulture Area. An estimated 1,035 farms were involved in grape production by the turn of the century.

Then, prohibition struck. In fact, Colorado adopted prohibition in 1916, four years prior to the rest of the nation. With that, grapes in the Grand Valley gave

way to the peach industry. They remained scarce until the early 1970s, when Colorado State University received a grant from the federal government and started looking into the viability of reestablishing wine grapes again. One of the test plots that they planted in 1974 was located directly in front of what is today Colorado Cellars.

Rick and Padte Turley, the owners of Colorado Cellars, can trace their ancestors' arrival in Colorado back as far as the grapes. Their own involvement in the state's viticulture industry coincides with its reemergence in the seventies.

One of the earliest of the Turley's ancestors arrived in present day Colorado via the Santa Fe Trail in 1824, while another co-founded Fort Pueblo (currently the town of Pueblo). From the early 1830s until his death in 1847, Simeon Turley, who grew and milled wheat, sold a particularly spicy brand of whiskey which was referred to as "Taos Lightening." The trappers who indulged in the alcohol claimed it made one feel as if he had been struck by lightning. While the present day Turley family does not provide the same fiery brew, they do run Colorado's oldest winery and sell wines under Colorado

Winery License No. 5 – the state's oldest license still in existence.

Rick and Padte began their journey towards vineyard ownership with the purchase of a fruit farm near Palisades in 1977. They began converting the orchards to vineyards and selling grapes to Colorado Mountain Vineyards, which had been founded by 11 investors using some of the original equipment and vines utilized by Colorado State University in their viticulture studies. Soon they took on sales for Colorado Mountain and were managing its statewide distribution.

The Colorado Mountain Vineyard became a sole proprietorship in 1986 and changed its name to Colorado Cellars. The new endeavor struggled and in 1989 Rick and Padte decided to purchase the winery themselves. Why did they decide to take a chance on it when others had already failed? There was actually a very practical reason according to Rick, "I bought the place because they weren't making any money and they couldn't buy my grapes anymore."

Both of the Turley's have a background in the wine distribution business so they know how retailers think. That has been critical to their success because they know what wines will be the most popular. However, it is not easy growing grapes in Colorado even if you know what will sell. At 4,700 to 6,400 feet above sea level, the Colorado vineyards are among the highest in the world. Intense sun during the summer and cool nights are great for grapes but the long, cold winters can be problematic. Improved vineyard management techniques are helping to solve that challenge and today, Colorado Cellars produces over 30 different types of wine including Port, Champagne, Whites, Reds, Rosé, Meads and a wide variety of fruit wines. In addition, since 1997 it has exclusively used grapes grown in the state of Colorado.

The couple forms what could be said to be the ideal wine making team. Padte is the winemaker (in fact, she was Colorado's first female winemaker!) and handles the running of the vineyard. "I love being out in the field or in the winery. I'm not doing the same work every day and I like that," she says. She brings a unique approach and perspective to her work. "You should never try to make things what they

are not. You nurture what you have, and I am conscious of how much I am requiring the vines to produce. You have to be careful about everything you do because we want the vines to last."

Rick, whom Padte refers to as her "co-conspirator," is the more outgoing of the two and heads up the marketing of the business. Acting as his own distributor, he makes his rounds personally and averages four days a week on the road. He often brings back feedback to help with the winemaking but his gift for promoting Colorado Cellars is obvious – 75 percent of their wine sales are made to retailers rather than through the winery directly.

Despite having the largest family-operated winery in Colorado, the pair continues to work hard to maintain their own business as well as to contribute to the success and growth of Colorado's wine industry. They have introduced two other labels in addition to Colorado Cellars – Rocky Mountain Vineyards, which has their best-selling wine, the off-dry RoadKill Red; and Colorado Mountain Vineyards under which they sell a champagne-style sparkling wine. The Turley's have also helped with the creation of

the Grand Valley American Viticulture Area in 1991 and the Colorado Wine Industry Development Board around that same time. From its rebirth with the Colorado Mountain Vineyard in 1978, the number of wineries in the state has grown to include over 120 today.

When asked about their wine, Padte says "People say our wines have a lot of finesse, that they have a beginning, middle and finish with character and complexity." The same could be said about the Turley family. They arrived on the Santa Fe Trail and supported the pioneers who were making a go of it on the frontier. They were fruit farmers when fruit was the only option. They foresaw the reemergence of an old industry and jumped into grapes when grapes were new again. They made their own way when there were few others investing in wineries and vineyards. And finally, they helped the nascent industry grow and thrive to become what it is today.

Cedar Hill Farm Company
Kuhlman Cellars

Yarn: *Single Sheep; Natural*
Functional, Exceptional, Rustic, Down-to-Earth, Organic

Wine: *2016 Hensell Rosé*
Floral, Perfumed, Refreshing, Complex, Fruit-Forward

The yarn is simple at first glance but further study reveals a luminescent glow which, when utilized with the highlighted pattern, produces a timeless beauty. The Rosé wine exhibits a pleasing blend of fruit flavors which is complex yet down to earth. Together, this pairing possesses a depth and grace which are traditional and elegant.

Cedar Hill Farm Company
Keya Kuhn

"I want magic! Yes, yes magic! I try to give that to people!"
Blanche – *A Streetcar Named Desire* by Tennessee Williams

In the Blue Mountains of Northeast Georgia, Stanley, Stella and Blanche are still striving to make magic but this time it is under the direction of Keya Kuhn. And they are sheep. The three were the start of what is today a flock that produces the *"Single Sheep"* yarn base, which is the pride of Cedar Hill Farm Company. Known for its luminosity and depth of color, this single-ply yarn is earthy and vivid and in many ways represents Keya herself. The raising of wool has helped to propel her down her artistic path as a designer, dyer, knitter and fiber farmer.

Taught to knit by her grandmother at age nine, she was fascinated by the thought that, with two sticks and some yarn, she could create something wearable. "I do what I do because of the inspiration from my grandmother to create beautiful, yet functional things and to grow my own everything," says Keya. "Crafting for me is simply a part of who I am, and if I wasn't

dyeing yarn, designing knitwear patterns or raising sheep, I would be doing something else artistically based."

Once set in motion, she continued to be an avid knitter (if she is sitting she is knitting!) but she always had the temptation to redesign or to alter the patterns she was using. With that urge always whispering in her ear, it was not long before she entered the world of pattern designing. Creating some popular knitting patterns, (including the *Strand Hill* cardigan for Knit Picks *Golden Morning Collection* and the *Palazzo Scarf* for the Knit Picks "2015 *Spring Accessories Collection*") set the groundwork for what Keya considers her favorite design to-date: the Cygnus Shawl.

It is a stunning piece with delicate details and an elegant drape designed specifically to highlight the luminosity and depth of Cedar Hill Farm's *Single Sheep* yarn base. Describing the piece's inception, Keya's excitement is obvious, "When the pattern first began circling my head, I had no idea how magnificent the final product would be. This particular shawl is one of the few items that I have knit that I can say is truly heirloom worthy.

It's just plain stunning and it is knit completely in yarn that I raised, myself."

Fun Fact:
The names of the colorways in Keya's Journey yarn base represent her bucket-list of travel destinations including Bali, Ellis Island, La Rue de Paris, Lisbon, Napa Valley, Rio, Sydney, Tokyo and Valley of Tears.

Which brings us back to Stanley, Stella and Blanche. In 2010, Keya convinced her husband to drive to South Carolina and pick up the three lambs as the start of a project to create her own natural, farm raised yarn. "I like the idea of dyeing, raising and sharing with the public a natural fiber with history" says Kuhn. Stanley is a Teeswater/Cormo crossbreed and the ladies are Corriedale/Finn crossbreeds. Together they have created a cross bred herd which produces a beautiful single-ply yarn that "you won't find anywhere else on the market simply because it is the result of the careful cross-breeding of four different breeds of sheep for the purpose of creating a yarn that is so luminous that it literally glows in the sunlight."

Keya's first foray into dyeing came as she was working as an English teacher. After an afternoon spent tie-dyeing shirts with students, she and a colleague started playing around in the art room with silk dye and later she spent a good bit of time in her kitchen with some Kool-Aid packets and a microwave oven. The resulting yarn became the first pair of socks she ever knit, and then there was no looking back. Today, the yarns of Cedar Hill Farm Company are vivid, earthy one-of-a-kind colorways, which perfectly highlight the natural world that serves as the inspiration for many of Keya's designs. According to Keya, she looks "...at what Nature had created and what man has created and I try to replicate

those color palettes." She describes her creative process as "...completely abstruse. It just comes or it doesn't come."

One thing that you will not see coming from Keya however is anything in yellow. Why? "I think that most people think dyers are in love with all colors, but I literally cannot stand the color yellow. You will see that most Indie dyers and all commercial yarn companies have a large selection of yarns that include the variations on the color yellow; I do not. It makes me cringe."

The location of Cedar Hill Farm is very apropos as the area has a long-standing commitment to fiber and was a major textile market in its earliest days with a large number of cotton mills, textile mills and clothing manufactures. The mills are gone but a number of small farms such as Cedar Hill carry on their legacy. Life on the Farm is busy and for Keya it includes taking care of her family, managing the farm (they raise sheep, horses, chickens, rabbits, dogs and cats – "Don't ask how many because it is an insane number" – as well as producing organic vegetables), running a business, designing knitwear, contributing to her community, sponsoring fiber

events (as well as teaching and vending at them throughout the year) and in her spare time, putting together her own collection of knitting patterns for her recently released book *South*.

In addition, there is her interest in yarn. "I'm a yarn addict. I have a stash that I will never knit through like all yarn addicts and then, I literally grow yarn in my back yard! Typically, I have several projects going at the same time. I think I currently have four sweaters, two or three pairs of socks, two blankets, a few hats and I do not even know what is in hibernation in the closet under the stairs. I have a project for every situation, meaning some are portable (car knitting, basketball game or tennis match knitting), some are weather specific (hot weather knitting or cold weather knitting), and some are for early morning, get-my-brain-going knitting, while others are intended to wind me down at the end of the day."

For someone so busy in the here and now, it can be challenging to think about what the future might hold, but Keya has some ideas. "I would like to expand the company as well as continue to produce knitting patterns." There has also been some talk about expanding their flock. And she would like a closet filled with her own hand knits. "Most of my knitting is done for the benefit of other people as gifts or custom requests or test knits for patterns I design and I would like to focus more of my attention on knitting for myself as a change of pace." Having come a long way from the little girl learning to knit by her grandmother's side, Keya Kuhn sums up her outlook simply and succinctly, "I'm living several of my childhood dreams all at once; so I'm content for now to revel in that."

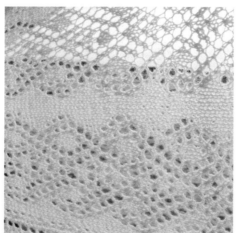

"Single sheep is intended to be used in every-day life. It holds its blocking incredibly well, is excellent for lace work and is also an ideal go-to for sweaters. I selected it for this project because I raise it, and that's pretty incredible if you ask me." - Keya

Cygnus Lace Shawl by Keya Kuhn

Kuhlman Cellars
Chris and Jennifer Cobb / Bénédicte Rhyne

It may not be as well known as some other wine producing regions in the United States, but Texas has a long history with wine. In fact, Franciscan priests in what is now Texas, needing wine for their Sacraments, planted the first vineyards in North America in the 1600s. In the late 1800s, Texas horticulturalist T.V. Munson grafted phylloxera-inflicted vitis vinifera from Europe to the pest-resistant native Texan rootstock, saving the world from one of the most devastating vineyard epidemics in history. While Chris and Jennifer Cobb do not have a goal of saving the world's vineyards, they are part of a growing agricultural movement aiming to put Texas wine on the map.

The couple visited the Napa Valley on their honeymoon and that is "where the magic began," says Jennifer. That fueled a shared lifelong passion for wine that led the Cobb's to start experimenting with growing vines at their Austin home while both were still part of the corporate world. It was not long before they found themselves purchasing a farm in the Texas Hill Country so that they had more room to grow more grapes. Like all good experiments, it took on a life of its own from there – first they managed a small estate vineyard and then decided to open a winery of their own.

"A life without wine is not complete"

In creating Kuhlman Cellars, the Cobb's wanted to ensure that they were able to highlight and pay homage to the land that inspires them and allows them and the other local winemakers to create something that is uniquely Texan. The most obvious example of this is the adoption of the name of Kuhlman Creek, which originates on their properly, for the name of their business. A more subtle example is found in their "idea that wine is supremely agricultural by nature, [building] a bond enjoyed from dirt to barrel to bottle." They "listen carefully to the terroir of Texas and what it is telling us about what to plant on a particular site," says Chris.

The Texas Terroir (the wind, rain, temperature, soil, elevation, etc. in a given region) is what allows Kuhlman Cellars, as well as other regional wineries, to create such distinct products.

In their corner of the Hill Country, they enjoy two AVA's (American Viticulture Areas) – Texas High Plains and Texas Hill Country. The High Plains have sandy soil, hot summers, low humidity and a large diurnal shift in temperature (from day to night). The large temperature shift is key to retaining acidity. Red wines made from High Plains fruit tend to be more subtle, offering soft tannins and a well-rounded mouthfeel while white wines can be extremely aromatic and delicate. The Hill Country has a narrower diurnal shift (making it harder to retain acidity), intense heat (leading to bigger tannins) and a soil tending towards clay and limestone (lending more minerals to the wine). Red wines from this region are more powerful and tannic with a greater mineral taste, often mimicking Old World style wines, while whites have a greater mineral profile and are very aromatic.

While this is all wonderful information, how were Chris and Jennifer to know what to do with this knowledge as they started their journey down the vine-bordered path? How do you even get started once you decide you want to grow grapes and make wine on a large scale? For the Cobb's, help came in the form of a farm neighbor – winemaker Bénédicte Rhyne.

Early on in her education in France, Ms. Rhyne developed an interest in science and the natural world. When combined with her love of travel and food, it was almost preordained that she become a wine maker. It was not an easy road however – graduating from l'Université de Dijon in 1987 with a degree in winemaking, she was only one of three women in the program that year. "I feel a lot of pride in the fact that more women are getting involved in the profession," she says as the number of women vintners continues to slowly expand. "Becoming a winemaker does not happen overnight. Studying, tasting and realizing that it is a lifetime learning experience requires a ton of humility" she advises.

Fun Fact:
Bénédicte's favorite wine is Champagne. Her grandfather let her suck on a Jordan almond dipped in Champagne on her baptism when she was a month old and she was hooked!

As her career has progressed, Bénédicte has been fortunate to train under the tutelage of renowned winemakers Jean Claude Berrouet (Ets.Jean-Pierre Moueix Libourne, France), Ross Spence (Matua Valley Wines, New Zealand) and Joel Peterson (Ravenswood, Sonoma, California).

In 2012, Bénédicte was approached by the Cobb's about working with them on the development of Kuhlman Cellars. "I liked their vision and what they were presenting to me and felt very compelled to join the venture," she says. With her unique background of Old World training and winemaking experience, combined with a passion for overcoming challenges in new regions, she was the perfect complement to the team.

When asked about her greatest success, Bénédicte replies without hesitation "my greatest success as a vintner has been to show that splendid wines can be produced in an area never thought of before such as Texas. With knowledge, wisdom, perseverance and a lot of humility, I am so proud to see that Mediterranean varietals are thriving in Texas Terroirs. Coming from Provence in France and having worked

through my life with Bordeaux grapes and California Zinfandel, I am delighted to see that all those varieties are doing extremely well in Texas." With an appreciation "that the product that I am making came from the earth and through the love and hard work of many, is being presented, shared and enjoyed", it is no wonder she ended up working with the Cobb's to create a focus on enhancing the connection of the earth to their wine.

It is not all work however, and Ms. Rhyne paints a delightful picture when asked about her time away from the winery. "I love cooking while my husband plays the piano and entertaining friends, sharing our passion for food, wine and music" she says with a smile.

As she looks forward to celebrating her 30th vintage as a winemaker, are there any changes in store? "I am fulfilled and happy with where I am at the moment and living the challenges of putting Texas on the wine map is extremely exhilarating," Bénédicte replies. Something that is sure to please not only the Cobb's and the team at Kuhlman Cellars but the rest of the Texas wine industry as well!

"We produce the Hensell Rosé every vintage but the 2016 was one of our most unique. With notes of ripe raspberry, strawberry, melon rind, white flowers and wet slate, the Hensell will both challenge and refresh the palate." - Jennifer

Hedgehog fibres
Hetta Glögg

Yarn: *Chubby; Fool's Gold*
Chunky, Black & White, Striking, Different, Special

Wine: *HETTA Glögg*
Warm, Spicy, Traditional, Family, Fun

The soft, squishy yarn is energetic and excited like a child with a brightly wrapped gift. The mulled wine is a fun, traditional recipe with a pleasant heat that spreads from your head to your toes. Together, this pairing is like a family gathering for the holidays - warm, fun, comfortable and happy.

Hedgehog fibres
Beata Jezek

Knitting legend Elizabeth Zimmerman had a motto: "Knit on, with confidence and hope, through all crises." This saying has provided comfort and inspiration to knitters around the globe and is something that Beata Jezek holds dear. In fact, she had it tattooed to her wrist so it is never far away and it has acted a rudder throughout her life. When asked how she handles challenging times, Beata replies, "Nothing is ever smooth sailing, but I don't like to dwell on negative things and if something is not working out, I just move on."

"Cast on all things!"

Originally from Slovakia, Beata has called Ireland home for over a decade and was living there in 2008, when the Irish economy experienced a downturn that resulted in the loss of her job. With a lot of time suddenly on her hands, she decided to take up knitting. As no teacher was handy, she turned to the Internet and was able to get started using all of the videos which she found there. Jumping straight in, her first project was a sock, something many knitters do not elect to take on until after they have mastered the basics. The results were mixed – the huge Christmas stocking sized piece wasn't exactly what she was hoping for ("I didn't know that gauge was something important to consider" she explains) but she fell in love with knitting from the first stitch.

Joining a local knitting group helped her to speed up her learning and connected her to the local craft community but straight away, she saw that there was going to be a problem with her new hobby. "In 2008, I couldn't find the colors that I was into available anywhere. Back then, hand dyed was much more limited and I felt I could do better than what was on the market. I always liked crafty things and working with my hands and I think I have a good color sense, so I thought yarn dyeing would be a great creative outlet. I don't remember the first color or product – at the beginning, I experimented a lot."

When she showed her experiments to her friends, they encouraged her to start her own business. With nothing to lose, she started Hedgehog fibres in 2008. The company name is derived from her last name, Jezek, which in Slovakian means 'Hedgehog.' Her vision at the time was quite simple, "I really wanted to create my own yarn line of soft, squishy yarns in beautiful colors. It's colors I want to knit with, colors I want to wear and the colors I can't live without." She placed her yarns on Etsy and hoped for the best. After her first sales started to come in and then she sold out of her inventory, she began to feel like she just might be on to something.

Today, Beata's artisan yarn and fiber dyeing studio provide a variety of colorful products to an enthusiastic following around the world. She is very selective about the bases that she uses and relies on her own high standards as a knitter as a benchmark. "I want the most buttery soft sock yarn, the shiniest silk blends, and the squishiest singles. As a knitter, I will only sell something I am happy to use." Beata likes all wool but prefers Merino for its versatility, softness and whiteness, which is important in achieving bright colors. She is fond of Blue Faced Leicester for its durability and also loves Mohair as a carry along yarn for fuzzy sweaters or held single for shawls. "Nobody does color on mohair like Hedgehog fibres!" she says with pride.

As one might suspect from someone who likes color, Ms. Jezek pays special attention to the colorways that Hedgehog fibres produces. "Our yarns tend to pool less, as the repeat is very short, often just one stitch per color. The colors are rich, complex and lively. Even our semi-solids consist of layers and layers of dye." And where does she find her inspiration? "I get this question a lot," she says. "This is my life, knitting, yarn and colors. Everything and anything can be an inspiration. I love coming up with new colors, techniques and applications. I am always thinking of the next thing, trying new ways of laying the dye on

Fun Fact:
Beata owns virtually every set of interchangeable needles on the market. She doesn't own any straight needles because she doesn't like using them.

yarn, new color combos. It's always the colors I'm into at the moment."

While Hedgehog fibres will not make any compromises in terms of quality and color, they also set a high standard on ethical and environmental considerations related to their products. They are 100% opposed to the practice of mulesing and ensure that their suppliers are only providing mulesing free stock to them. All of their yarn is sourced from South America and produced using working conditions that are not exploitative. The company also uses non-toxic acid dyes, ensures that they have virtually zero dye waste and employs a biodegradable setting agent. For shipping purposes, they re-use boxes when they can and all of their packaging is purchased locally.

While Hedgehog's growth has required a lot of dedication, discipline and effort, Beata still does manage to carve out a little time for herself. When she is not involved with Hedgehog fibres activities, you can find her doing a bit of gardening, knitting or drinking wine. "Sometimes I knit or garden while drinking wine!" she says happily. Some of her favorite types of knitting projects are

shawls and accessories because gauge is still not something that she takes into consideration much. Above all, she loves to create with color. "One of my own patterns – Outline – is probably my favorite because you can get very creative with the colors and the construction is very simple."

With color always on her mind and a determination to continue to grow her business, what is next for Beata and Hedgehog fibres? "We are looking to expand further but everything takes so much time and nothing ever happens fast enough for my liking. I would really like it if I didn't need to sleep – I'd get so much done!" Are there any particular challenges that she foresees along the way? "No, if I want to do something, then I do it!" she says. A sentiment that Elizabeth Zimmerman would certainly applaud.

Thrice by Lisa Mutch

Hetta Glögg
Darren Davidowich

The tradition of spiced wine began during the 2nd century with Romans sweetening their wine and adding flowers and herbs. As Rome expanded its empire throughout Europe, its legions brought wine and viticulture with them along with their recipes.

During the middle ages, spiced wine became very popular across Europe. Adding herbs to mediocre wine improved its taste and was thought to impart healing properties to the drink. The Swedish king, Gustav Vasa loved a blend of red wine, sugar, honey and spices. Lutendrank, a spiced wine which was not overly sweet, was the favorite drink of King Erik XIV of Sweden; he had 210 jugs of it produced for his coronation in 1561.

Fun Fact:
In the 1500s, glögg was sold using the name 'Hippocras'; playing off of the name Hippocrates, the famous Greek physician often referred to as 'the father of medicine.'

In later years, spiced wines, while still available, fell out of favor in many parts of Europe but their popularity remained high in the Nordic countries. The word glögg, derived from the word glödga meaning "to heat up", first appeared in the early 1600s and during the 1890s became a Swedish Christmas tradition. Every wine merchant had their own blend, with imaginative and creative holiday labels to entice buyers, and the drink became a welcome addition to late afternoon or early evening holiday parties and gatherings. That remains the case today and every Christmas over 5 million liters of glögg are consumed in Sweden.

That Nordic holiday drink has now made its way to New York's Hudson Valley, where Darren Davidowich and his family business, HETTA Glögg, are putting a new spin on an old tradition and introducing glögg to a new and appreciative audience.

The idea to sell glögg was born, fittingly, at a holiday party on Christmas Eve 2009. Amy Davidowich had prepared a glögg using a family recipe brought from Norway in the 1920s by her great grandparents. The family was

enjoying the drink when her brother-in-law Darren was struck with inspiration and asked if he might use the recipe. "He already had a business plan in his mind" says Amy. Soon, the family started to tweak the mixture, using brandy in place of vodka for a smoother taste and experimenting with the use of cinnamon, raisins, cardamom, and orange peel.

At first, the venture was a part-time operation; the family continued to pursue a variety of professional careers (Darren was, and still is, a real estate developer for instance), while perfecting their recipe, developing their production capabilities, designing bottles and packaging and all of the other activities required to build a business. Darren's brother Kevin and his father-in-law Gary undertook the monumental task of deciphering the New York State approval process for alcohol manufacturing and distribution and obtaining the proper licensing – a task which required over three years to complete. The family decided to use HETTA (Swedish for "heat") as its company name and chose the Dala horse as its logo because it symbolizes hospitality, friendship and good will.

Fun Fact:
Mulled wine is normally served warm. The warm liquid raises the temperature of the drinkers mouth and stomach slightly and because alcohol is a vasodilator, it forces blood outward to the skin, producing a warm feeling which is especially pronounced if consuming the drink after coming in out of the cold weather.

With everything in place, the glögg produced by HETTA finally reached store shelves in November of 2013, just in time for the holidays. This updated version of mulled wine starts with a port wine custom made for them in the Finger Lakes Region of New York State. They then add cinnamon, orange peel, cardamom and raisins (all organic and locally sourced) and allow it to steep, according to Davidowich. The final ingredient is brandy, which brings the ABV (alcohol by volume) to 21.9 percent. The glögg is then heated and bottled warm. The end result is full of bright fruit, a pleasant sweetness and spice – very much tasting and smelling like the holidays.

This American twist on a Nordic glögg is certainly a welcome addition to any winter festivity and is typically heated and sipped out of a small glass. The company, however, is not satisfied with providing a holiday treat and they are quick to point out that HETTA is perfect for the colder months and there are many additional ways to enjoy their drink. "In champagne, on the rocks, in tea, over vanilla ice cream," Kevin Davidowich, Amy's husband, ticks off all of the creative variations that they have tried. "Once, we gave bottles to some student chefs at the Culinary Institute of America and they served it as a reduction with duck."

This traditional drink is slowly catching on and gaining in popularity. Now available in stores in New York, New Jersey, Vermont and Connecticut, production has steadily increased and HETTA is becoming much more than the part time venture that it started out as and the family is excited to share their tradition with a much wider audience. "Growing up, this was a part of Christmas and I made it out of love for my grandmother," Amy says. "Now my parents and husband and brother-in-law have taken the family recipe and done so much. I'm flattered to see now what it's become and wish my great grandmother and grandfather could see it."

Served as a welcoming beverage to arriving guests, it is easy to see how glögg would be a great addition to any holiday gathering. And HETTA, with its Dala horse representing hospitality, friendship and good will, is excited to help you with an introduction.

Elemental Affects
Olalla Vineyard & Winery

Yarn: *Shetland Fingering; Black, Emsket (grey), Sea Foam*
Deep, Natural, Primitive, Fine, Soft

Wine: *2015 Golubok*
Jammy, Fruit-Forward, Refreshing, Unusual, Mouth-Filling

The yarn is soft and fine and can trace its ancestry back to the earliest days of the British Isles. The wine is unusual in both its taste and creation; unexpectedly fruity and aged in the tradition of ancient Greeks and Romans. This pairing draws upon and highlights the ancient lineage of yarn and wine and provides us with a pleasant echo of our past.

Elemental Affects
Jeane deCoster

Jeane deCoster learned to spin when she was in her late twenties and living in Southern California. It was a tremendous stress reliver while working in a very demanding industry. She spent most of her career in IT but her Bachelor's Degree is in Fashion Design and she had been interested in knitting as a hobby from a young age. As she remembers, around 2005, "I saw the writing on the wall with my career being metered and shifted overseas, so I started looking into resources available to help leverage both my hobby and technical skill sets into a viable business expertise."

She began with a distance-learning program in New Zealand and took a week-long dyeing seminar from Allen Fannin at Syracuse University. This combination of spinning and dyeing started her thinking about the creation of a hand-dyed yarn company. While living and working in New York, she continued experimenting in her tiny kitchen until tragedy struck and she was prompted to take the next step. On September 11, 2001, like many others in the City, Jeane witnessed the terrorist attacks on the World Trade Center, as well as other locations, and started to take a harder look at the future. "I decided it was time to leave New York and take the leap into starting my own business," she explains. "So, I moved back home and started putting my business plan together."

Jeane's early spinning efforts saw her working with both Shetland and Romney fleece and she was fascinated by what could be done with the rustic, naturally colored wool. Primarily only available from overseas, she was convinced that an affordable Shetland yarn could be made in the United States. Many in the industry however, met this plan with skepticism. "They said that we couldn't make a viable commercial yarn from such a small, colored, primitive sheep," says Jeane. Luckily, she was determined. "I have that DNA that rebels when somebody tells me that something can't be done!"

It was also lucky that she had taken spinning classes with Judith MacKenzie and the two had become good friends. Judith introduced Jeane to a friend of hers in Montana, who had just acquired what seemed to be the largest Shetland flock in the United States. The rancher had obtained the sheep for two reasons – she thought that they were cute and more importantly, she was in desperate need of weed control! Focused on her ranch, she was not interested in selling the individual fleeces to handspinners and Jeane was able to reach an agreement to purchase her entire clip every year to begin developing her yarn.

With that done, Jeane set about learning about shearing, skirting, sorting, classing the wool and turning it into a commercially viable yarn. Until that time, Shetland yarn was only available as an import or from hand-spinning flocks produced through small custom processors or mills. What she needed was a commercial mill that would process the wool into a yarn at a price that would allow it to be affordable. Eventually she was able to locate a mill and worked with them to achieve her dream of producing Shetland yarn. However, while Shetland yarn was her goal, it was actually not her first product.

While she was waiting for her first yarn to come from the mill, her good friend Judith introduced her to her first Wool Pool and she snapped up several hundred pounds of amazingly long, soft and lustrous Romney fiber. As Jeane recalls, "A little earlier, Deb Menz's book about blending dyed spinning fiber (*Color in Spinning*) came out and it inspired me to dye pounds of Romney locks in primary colors." She thought that if she showed samples of the product spun in different color blends, customers would snap up the dyed locks. "The idea was a bomb (failure). Customers preferred to have their fiber already blended, so my next product was the same Romney fiber dyed in primary colors but carded into roving." This product was more successful and kept her going while she continued to develop her Shetland yarn.

Shetland sheep come in a wide range of colors including a whole range of cool grays to black and light warm gray brown to a really dark brown. "Every year I work with these sheep and the shearing team and clean and sort the fleece into a manageable range of natural colors – colors that both provide a range of natural colors for the knitter and to me as a dyer," explains Jeane. The natural shades of yarn are scoured lightly using solar power and a simple detergent and then they are spun at the mill.

After the Shetland and Romney yarns were developed, Jeane needed to expand her product portfolio with a soft wool and elected to add Cormo. "In the process, the opportunity to develop a yarn using U.S. Merino and Chinese Mulberry silk came along. It took me a while to accept that it was a good idea and in the process, modify my own mission statement to accommodate the idea of U.S. yarns with 'bling' or really, allowing myself to use imported raw materials when they provide a specific quality to the yarn I am designing that I can't get otherwise."

Today, Jeane's company, Elemental Affects, is focused on "hand-dyed, breed specific, international yarn – made in the U.S." Asked for clarification, Jeane replies, "It's kind of a weird phrase but it means that I buy my raw materials (fiber) as close to the source as possible – in most cases, that means working directly with the breeders. I then work with our few remaining commercial mills to design yarns that express the unique qualities of the fiber and result in yarns that will be pleasing to hand knitters and weavers."

Those unique qualities also resulted in her company name – Elemental Affects. After finding that "Elemental Effects" was unavailable as a web domain name, Jeane wondered about replacing 'effects' with 'affects.' When learning that affect means to touch the feelings of or move emotionally, she appreciated the deeper meaning. In her own words, "Elemental Affects yarns are made with natural fibers such as wool, silk, etc. and are created in the hope of touching the feelings of knitters and evoking a wonderful emotional response."

What's next for Jeane and Elemental Affects? "When I started in the business, I was pretty sure that I wouldn't last through the first 5 years of a new business," she says. "Once I did that, I just kept going." And with her business continuing to grow, it looks like she will be going for some time to come.

"My grandfather and both my parents worked at See's Candies, a famous Southern California candy company. My parents actually met while working there – he as a truck driver and she as a temporary chocolate dipper. My grandfather worked there all his life until he finally retired as the manager of the shipping department. When one of the See brothers started a vineyard in Napa, California, Gramps was asked to "vineyard sit" during the summers when the owner was vacationing elsewhere. One of my favorite memories is spending the summer on the vineyard with my grandfather. I was introduced to many exotic things like domestic peacocks and Rhodesian Ridgeback hounds. But I think that my favorite thing was lazing around the swimming pool and making fizzy peach sodas from the yummy white peaches that grew by the pool and soda water from a dispenser. I have very fond memories of those bubbles. I felt like a very exotic (and cool) teenager and imagined away many lazy summer days at that vineyard. As I was creating and knitting this pattern, my mind often wandered back to those times in the vineyard with my grandfather." - Jeane

Bubbles by Jeane deCoster

Olalla Vineyard & Winery
Mary Ellen Houston and Stuart Chisholm

Ever since Mary Ellen Houston and her husband Stuart Chisholm were married, they wanted to run a business together. Stuart, from Edinburgh, Scotland, and Mary Ellen, a Pittsburgh native, met in Seattle in 2011 and were married in December of 2012. A year or so thereafter, they began looking for a venture that would suit their needs. After evaluating several opportunities, they discovered that Olalla Vineyard was for sale. Being wine enthusiasts, they decided to investigate. It was a small, family owned winery with a Croatian Heritage and after seeing the wondrous beauty of the location, Mary Ellen and Stuart decided this was the place for them and became vineyard owners in December 2015.

Fun Fact:
Mary Ellen and Stuart love riding motorcycles in their free time.

There were, of course, some challenges to overcome. Neither of them knew much about winemaking or running their own business. However,

they jumped in and were determined to make it succeed. The first step was bringing Matthew Loso on board as a consultant and winemaker. He is a master winemaker and was the original owner of Matthews Cellars in Woodinville, WA – one of the most well-known and well-respected wineries in Washington State. He taught the new owners the many aspects of winemaking with hands-on lessons. Stuart and Mary Ellen also attended courses in vineyard management via the WSU Extension and plunged into extensive reading on wines and wine-making.

The new venture had many positive aspects. The first was that it was already an existing business and had been producing estate wines from grapes grown and nurtured on the premises. The vineyard in Olalla was growing a number of red and white varietals including Pinot Noir, Pinot Gris, Gewürztraminer, Viognier, Syrah, Merlot, Cabernet Franc and Golubok.

Golubok is an uncommon varietal in the USA but is Olalla's flagship wine. It is a deep purple varietal with a Cabernet Sauvignon parentage, hails from Eastern Europe and is

particularly well suited to the Puget Sound climate with its cooler temperatures and damp growing conditions. As Mary Ellen explains, "Golubok thrives in these conditions and is used to having 'wet feet.' It is a medium to full-bodied red wine, very fruit-forward berry flavors and low on tannins and acidity. I like to call it 'the red wine for white wine drinkers'." As one of the few vineyards in the state of Washington or elsewhere in the USA growing Golubok, combined with the small batch production, Olalla sells out of each vintage produced.

The second aspect of the vineyard that has helped to set it apart is its use of handcrafted, Italian clay amphorae in the winemaking process which binds the grape fermentation to the earth from

which the grapes originated. Amphora are clay pots that were used in wine production by the ancient Greeks and Romans, as far back as 800 B.C. They have been used to transport and store a variety of products both liquid and dry but are primarily associated with wine. The clay pots can be used for aging wines and the porosity of the clay increases the oxygen exposure of wines while they age. Oxygen accelerates the tertiary flavor development, which includes softening tannins and increasing aromas of nuts, baked fruit and chocolate. Famously used by the Greeks and Romans for centuries, this ancient wine-making method creates clean, fruit forward wine that replicates the best of the classic old world style vintages. Modern winemakers who have switched to amphorae say that

the vessels produce the purest expression of their grape and vineyard areas.

While Mary Ellen and Stuart are quickly learning all the intricacies of their new venture, every day still holds new challenges. Mary Ellen recalls their first harvest required the newbie wine makers to literally be quick on their feet. "October 2016 was our first harvest and Stuart and I were picking Pinot Noir, all 303 pounds of it, and it was getting late in the day. The sun was setting and we were getting ready to put the grapes into the 'de-stemmer'. After turning the machine on, it appeared that the mechanism was somehow jammed. That late in the day, we had no time to investigate so we had no choice but to stomp the grapes ourselves – all 303 pounds! I sanitized my feet and jumped into a stainless-steel bin and my husband started chucking grapes in. I stomped (ala 'I Love Lucy') for two hours straight! Months later, we sent in a sample of the Pinot Noir to the lab for testing and found out that it was a perfectly clean and well-balanced Pinot Noir! It was truly a labor love."

While the husband and wife team is still very new to the business, they have no regrets

about their choice. "We absolutely love what we do," says Mary Ellen. "Working in the tasting room, I get the opportunity to meet some amazing people. I love introducing new wines to our customers and since I am a very social person, it is the perfect job for me!" What is the most satisfying aspect of their new jobs? "The most satisfaction is seeing the fruits of our labor (pun intended!) and seeing our patrons enjoying themselves, relaxing at one of our tables, listening to music or strolling around, whilest enjoying delicious wines in our little piece of Heaven on Earth."

The Woolen Rabbit
Dry Creek Vineyard

Yarn: *Dove; Water Study*
Elegant, Sophisticated, Crisp, Fine, Drape

Wine: *2014 Old Vine Zinfandel*
Historic, Aromatic, Flavor, Complex, Refined

The yarn and colorway convey a classic elegance which, when combined with a pattern of delicate lace-work, produces a piece best worn for a night out on the town. The Zinfandel comes from some of the oldest vines in California and is wonderfully complex and sophisticated. This combination transports one to a time of formal attire, dinner clubs, and evenings filled with grace and refinement.

The Woolen Rabbit
Kim Kaslow

Artists first discovered the towering peaks and raw beauty of the White Mountains of New Hampshire in the early 1900s. One of the first to sketch the peaks was Thomas Cole, the founder of the Hudson River School of painting. Even though the area was still relatively remote and not easily accessible, others were soon making the trek to attempt to capture the power of the dramatic vistas and ultimately, over 400 artists would paint scenes in the Mountains over the next century. One of the most famous was Benjamin Champney who purchased a house in North Conway, New Hampshire and established it as the defacto center of what was the first artist colony in North America (captured by Winslow Homer in his 1868 painting entitled *Artists Sketching in the White Mountains*.) While not subject to the same artistic scrutiny as they once were, the White Mountains still provide a magnificent landscape and serve as inspiration for resident fiber artist Kim Kaslow.

"Dream big!"

Like many others, Kim was introduced to knitting at an early age by her grandmother. As Kim recalls, "She taught me to knit, purl, cast on and cast off and said that with those skills, I could knit anything I wanted. And she was right." Kim went through some starts and stops with her knitting over the years and did not really become a serious knitter until her early 20's. Following the loss of a child and while pregnant with her second child, she needed something to keep her busy and dug out her needles. She started first with crocheting and then moved on to knitting, eventually becoming skilled enough to be hired as a knitter of sample sweaters for a company in New York City called Merino. She has not put down her knitting since.

Sometime later, Kim was working as a waitress with a friend and they would both bring their knitting to occupy their breaks and slow times. Her friend would also bring her drop spindle along and, noticing Kim's interest, brought along an extra one for her to take home and try. So began one of the most frustrating weekends of Kim's life. "There is a reason they call it a drop spindle," she says with a chuckle. She returned it on Monday with a simple question "Why in the world would you ever want to do this?" However, while the drop spindle proved to be an epic failure, when Kim was introduced to a spinning wheel shortly thereafter, it was a completely different experience for her. "I was very comfortable from the start and absolutely loved it."

She took to spinning naturally and it was just a short hop from there to obtaining some rabbits to provide her with raw material. "It started with one angora rabbit, which multiplied, as rabbits will, into a small herd which produced wonderful fiber to blend with wools," she says. Those Marino/Angora blends resulted in Kim's business "The Woolen Rabbit."

Kim focused on her fiber creations for a number of years and gradually became interested in dyeing. As she became more comfortable with the dyeing process, she transitioned over to working with manufactured yarns as they gave her a cleaner, more reliable product. She worked hard to develop a method that would prevent pooling and really wanted her yarns to look as beautiful in the final fabric as they did on the skein. She was able to achieve this and her business slowly began to grow as she worked on it part time while her children grew up. Ultimately, she was able to turn what started out as a hobby into a full time career.

A lot of Kim's color inspiration comes from nature and she tends to favor earthy colors for the simple reason that those are the colors she prefers to wear. She is also quick to add that she "has been fortunate to work with some fabulous designers over the years and collaborate on inspirational projects with them." For example, she and longtime friend Anne Hanson have similar color sensibilities and have teamed up a number of times. "Anne will send me a photo of something that inspired her design and ask me create a specific color. For her sweater 'Leaving' she sent me a picture of a bunch of dying hostas," says Kim laughing. "For a more recent project she sent a photo of roses on a rose bush with a hint of chocolate in them."

In addition to her other work, Kim has been experimenting with block printing fabrics and now offers a variety of soaps, lotions and knitting bags in her store. Has she become tired of dyeing? Absolutely not. "I am looking at other ways to create in a way that is a little less stressful – dyeing can be very tough on the body." Moreover, artistic brains need a creative outlet, Kim notes. As is the nature with crafty people, she enjoys a wide variety of pursuits including weaving, sewing, quilting and of course spinning, which she is still passionate about. "I'm very blessed to own some amazing spinning wheels from real artists."

Kim is also working on a new edition of her yarn club, which she is reviving by popular demand after a hiatus. "I love to research things and come at colors and design from both an art perspective and historical perspective when I do a yarn club," she says. And what better place to do that than in the White Mountains of New Hampshire which have inspired artists for generations.

Meadow by Paulina Popiolek

"I was working with Anne Hanson on a project to create a yarn for a pattern she created based on the inspiration of the 1920s dancer, Isadora Duncan. In researching Ms. Duncan, to find a name for this yarn color, I spent some time watching her dance videos. Anne had requested a pastel blue/green, the shades of beach glass, which was a popular color in the 20s. As I watched the dances, 'The Water Study Solo' struck a cord with me. So full of movement, like the ebbs and tides of the ocean...a place dear to my heart." - Kim

Dry Creek Vineyard
The Stare Family

The Dry Creek General Store has been a fixture in Healdsburg, CA since 1881. It has been used as a stagecoach stop, feed store, bait shop, general mercantile, barbershop, bar and during Prohibition, there was bootlegging in the cellar. Regardless of its stated function, it has always served as a gathering place for local farmers to discuss the topics of the day, share information and give their opinion of the goings on in their little part of the world. One can only imagine their comments on the day that Dave Stare moved in across the road, ripped out the old, run down prune orchard and started planting Sauvignon Blanc.

"There will always be people that appreciate a more artisan approach to life" - Don Wallace

Dave was educated at the Massachusetts Institute of Technology and worked for the B&O Railroad for a number of years before he discovered his true calling. In 1970, he spent two weeks in France traveling through the wine country of Burgundy and Bordeaux, sampling the wines and investigating the vineyards and something just clicked – he came home from that trip knowing that he had to make wine in the style of the Loire Valley. His immediate plan was to move his family to France, build a chateau and get to work but fate intervened in the form of an article in the Wall Street Journal profiling the burgeoning wine industry in California. The next thing the family knew, they were being loaded into their mint green station wagon and heading across the country to begin a great new adventure.

Upon arriving on the West Coast, Dave enrolled at the University of California at Davis as a graduate student in winemaking and started to learn everything he could about his new profession. On the weekend, he scouted the area for a place to make his dream a reality. As he recalls, "it became fairly obvious that Northern Sonoma County had a history of winemaking and grape growing for over 120 years." During one of these trips, Dave came upon the old orchard across the road from the Dry Creek General Store and thought it would be the perfect location for his vineyard.

With a location established, he then needed to determine what types of grapes to plant. Thinking back to his inspiration, the Loire Valley, he immediately thought Sauvignon Blanc would be the ideal choice. After speaking with local farmers and vineyard managers however, he started to receive the same advice over and over. "They told me Sauvignon Blanc would never grow in the Dry Creek Valley," he says. Daughter Kim confirms, "I remember being a young girl and the farmers in the Valley telling my father that he was crazy." But the self-described, "stubborn Easterner" was determined to go ahead with his plan and in 1972 founded Dry Creek Vineyard, the first new winery to be established in the Dry Creek Valley since Prohibition.

With hindsight, son-in-law Don Wallace knows that Dave made the correct choice. "It was lucky that he had the idea. Napa had already set the stage for Cabernet. Zinfandel was here but it was more like an Italian old red wine – a farmer's blend. Sauvignon Blanc provided credibility and an international awareness to this little 16 mile long valley that we call home." The wines produced by Dry Creek Vineyard quickly started to gain a following and David became a leader in what was soon a rapidly expanding wine industry in Sonoma County.

Today the winery owns 185 acres of certified sustainable vineyards and produces Dry Chenin Blanc, Sauvignon Blanc, Chardonnay, Zinfandel, Cabernet Sauvignon and Meritage blends. Daughter Kim, who grew up on the vineyard before heading off to San Francisco State University, returned in 1986 as the Director of Marketing. One of her first contributions was the creation of Dry Creek Vineyard's iconic nautical labels. "Sailing has always been a passion of our family," says Kim. "Putting sailboats on the label was kind of a crazy thing, when you think about the brand name 'Dry Creek.' Having sailboats on the label conveys two things: our passion for sailing and our passion for wine. Those are the things we love most besides family."

In 2013, Kim was named the President of Dry Creek Vineyard following her husband Don in that position. She is determined that her family's winery will stay in the family and wants to honor her father's legacy of producing wines that consistently over deliver and provide great enjoyment for Dry Creek Vineyard's legions of fans worldwide. "Competition is at an all-time high in our industry so being true to our wines, our vineyards and the terroir of our region is more important than ever before," says Kim. A sentiment that Don seconds: "There is a reason why Dry Creek Valley is a strong hope for family owned wineries and that is because it is so distinctive. Because of the complexity of the climate conditions that are here, the wines are seamless, balanced and have a broad spectrum of flavor compounds that make the wines fascinating to taste. And that's a really special thing about this place."

Started by a stubborn Easterner determined to bring a piece of the Loire Valley to northern California despite what the "old-timers" thought, Dry Creek Vineyard has blossomed into a realization of the dreams that Dave Stare carried with him as he drove his family across America all those years ago. It has built its reputation by providing "something special" in the bottle which keeps visitors coming back for more, a commitment that the family's second generation continues to aspire to. "There is something connective about wine," says Kim. "To see people enjoying our wines, making friends with them and having that connectivity between us and our wines and our customers is the most remarkable feeling."

"During harvest, our Old Vine Zinfandel lots always show a distinct aroma and flavor profile. Once bottled, the perfumed nuances and dried herbal components shine through. At first swirl, bay leaf and white pepper leap from the glass balanced by deep layers of plum and cocoa. The complexity of our Old Vine Zinfandel lies in the spice notes that are unique to these historic properties. Refined and balanced, the wine integrates seamlessly on the palate, offering a broad array of currants, black cherry, raspberry and toasty oak notes." - Kim

Bedhead Fiber
Breakwater Vineyards

Yarn: *Hand-spun, Alpaca and Corriedale; Naturally Dyed*
Comforting, Healing, Buzzy, Boozy, Warm

Wine: *Bee's Knees Mead*
Light, Sweet, Crisp, Finish, Surprising

The yarn is soft and springy, all natural, hand made and deeply connected to nature. The wine is a mead - sweet and surprisingly light with a finish that is bright and crisp. Both are testaments to the role that Mother Nature (and her bees!) plays in providing us with these special gifts. Together, they are like a fun walk in the garden on a pleasant spring day - colorful, happy and alive.

Bedhead Fiber
Kelli Thoumsin

Kelli Thoumsin graduated college with an unusual goal in mind – to learn to grow food. "I was raised in Arizona where it's difficult to sustainably grow anything besides succulents and cacti," she explains. She left her home to start learning how to farm in Europe. On her first farm, the woman who owned and ran the operation patiently taught her how to knit. During her breaks, Kelli would sit outside and knit next to the farm dogs and goats, tension way too tight, splitting every knit and somehow creating extra stitches, all to the amusement of her teacher. Nevertheless, guided by her teacher's philosophy of "to learn, you do," slowly but surely she progressed and a passion for knitting was born.

One week she was sent to the big city of Volos' weekly market to find yarn and returned with a vibrant green polyester blend that was "just awful." She started on a scarf as well as a quest to find better quality yarn. In particular, with her interest in sustainable farming, she was determined to avoid using highly processed, synthetic yarns with unknown origin. When life led her to New York

and then on to Oregon, Kelli began researching the history of the textile industry and quickly realized she could utilize the plants that surrounded her as a natural and sustainable source of dyes.

"I believe in the power of plants"

Archaeologists have found evidence of textile dyeing dating back to the Neolithic period and in China, dying with plants, barks and insects has been traced back more than 5,000 years. While Kelli did not realize it at the time she was learning to knit, Greece has a very long history with dyed textiles as well – Homer even mentions dyes in some of his writings. Utilizing wool primarily, the Greeks used a variety of different materials to produce dye for their clothing including oak bark to produce brown, the roots of the herb madder for pink, the stalks of weld for yellow and dried woad leaves for the color blue.

Once in Oregon, Kelli started to forage for mushrooms and plants that she could harvest sustainably herself. "I found joy in dyeing yarn from household by-products," she explains, "like carrot tops and foraged

horsetail. After reading about the beloved cochineal bug, I gave that a go as well. Not a huge fan of pinks, I crushed the bug in a mortar and pestle and was enamored – I think I dyed five skeins from 10 grams of cochineal. I was in love. This pink wasn't like other pinks."

Kelli combined this passion for dyeing and the natural world with her quest to find better yarn to form Bedhead Fiber in 2017. Reflecting her beliefs, all of the dyestuffs she uses are harvested directly by her, other fiber and fungal lovers, fair trade or other certified farms and sourced as locally as possible. The company only sources wool from US grown and milled operators with a focus on Pacific Northwest farms. "I believe we must support farmers, makers, and creators in our communities," she says. While Kelli thinks that "foraging

and gardening most of my own materials is a bit rare" it may also be a sign of things to come. "With people becoming more aware of environmental issues, I think it's only a matter of time before people find more environmentally friendly methods for everyday objects and habits." Natural dyeing with plants and flowers is easier on the environment; using significantly less water and being nontoxic, harmful chemicals do not end up in waterways. With the fashion and textile industries being the second largest producer of harmful wastes right behind the petroleum industry, any step away from those processes is significant. It is this "slow fashion" movement that Kelli hopes to raise awareness of. "I'm seeing a lot more people planting dye gardens," she says hopefully.

Is it more challenging to create and use natural dyes while sourcing locally, seasonally and ethically? Certainly. "There aren't a whole lot of standard color recipes out there for natural dyers, so you're a bit on your own," Thoumsin explains. "Tried and tested recipes can yield different colors based off of the dye source, the season it was harvested, the health of the animal, etc. But if I end up with an unexpected or unwanted color, natural dyes lend themselves favorably to overdyeing." While this may sound challenging on a small scale, the unpredictable nature of the dyes can be even more problematic when trying to scale up a color to be recreated over and over for a business such as Bedhead Fiber. "The single dye lots of yarn usually are from small batches of items that I've

foraged or overdyed skeins," says Kelli. "I've only started to develop color lines this year so the process for that has been a little different – a lot more manipulation with the necessity of being able to recreate the color over and over."

Thus far, in its short existence, Bedhead Fiber has focused on naturally dyed fiber and hand spun yarn. When asked if the additional labor and time required to produce these is worth it, Kelli has a ready answer. "All my yarns are special to me. I devote hours to them in order to obtain something that someone else can create into something they cherish. Helping to facilitate that is wonderful." In addition, she "loves the process. The plants that I have ethically harvested are tactile, real, alive, and have so much to offer. The ritual of harvesting, scouring, mordanting, dyeing, and winding has been very grounding." And as long as she is "learning by doing" as advised by her old knitting teacher, Kelli will continue to explore the natural world around her and work to make it a better place.

Quick Knit Hat by Cynthia Spencer

"When we were told our pairing would be a mead, I immediately went back to when I worked on an apiary in Finland and drank homemade mead out of saved wine and beer bottles. I felt warm, happy, orange yellow. (Probably the mead!) - Kelli

Pollinator Project
Chelsea Thoumsin

Bonus Feature: *The Polinator Project is dedicated to raising awareness and helping to preserve bees and other pollinators. (And YES - Kelli and Chelsea are sisters!)*

Pollinator Project was born in Philadelphia in 2015 from the dedicated efforts of Chelsea Thoumsin. Chelsea had begun learning about bees and mentoring as a beekeeper in 2013. Within a year, she was keeping her own bees. "I was fascinated with how the colonies organized themselves, their behavior as a super-organism and genetic hierarchy. Of course, the prospect of harvesting honey was exciting, but I was lured to it to learn and to hopefully help them thrive," she explains.

As more and more people discovered that she had beehives, a bit of a rarity in urban Philadelphia at the time, Chelsea began to field many questions about honeybees. Specifically, folks wanted to know what they could do to help if they could not keep bees themselves. "I would

say, 'Plant pollinator friendly flowers," says Chelsea, "since we know that one of the main reasons honeybees (and other pollinators) are struggling to survive is due to a lack of food." The conversation would progress to types of flowers, growing conditions, and so on, but she could tell that she was losing some people along the way in the conversation. "That's when I decided to create a wildflower seed packet that was minimal in cost and maintenance but made a difference."

Could such a simple idea – planting flowers – really make a difference? There are over 4000 species of native bees in the United States alone and bees are the most predominant pollinators of flowering plants in nature. Technically, honeybees are not native to the U.S.; they originally came from Europe along with the early colonists but quickly became a critical part of the pollination process in the New World. In recent years, the honeybee populations have been in decline due to

a combination of infectious pathogens, malnutrition, stress and pesticides. Planting flowers that produce pollen and nectar, especially during the months when crops are not blooming, helps provide nutrition to honeybees. With diverse food sources, pollinators are better equipped to fend off disease, pathogens and the effects of stress.

Native bees can often fill the pollination needs of many crops where honeybees may be absent, although native bees live in significantly smaller communities than their Apis mellifera counterparts. In fact, there was a time when native bees and wild honeybees performed all of a farmers pollinating needs due to the presence of natural areas nearby. These natural areas provided nesting sites, food and protection. With changes in agricultural techniques and landscapes, native bee habitats and forage near farms have been greatly reduced. Two ways to combat this are to preserve or create diverse bee habitats, which include water, areas for nesting or egg-laying and secure over-wintering sites. Flowers that provide food are also critical. Not only will planting wildflowers feed bees, but they will also attract more pollinators to your garden and increase its yield.

Pollinator Project seed packets contain around 500 non-GMO seeds from a variety of wildflowers that will grow in stressful urban conditions such as low water, high heat and blazing sun. "They would grow in a sidewalk crack if they had to," Thoumsin says.

As an activist-entrepreneur, Chelsea is driven by her passion. "I care about pollinators, a lot, and I care a lot about the natural world," she says. However, she does have sales and business concerns to worry about as well. "I often find myself wondering if I'm doing enough, especially if sales are slow for any period of time. Then I realize that a person can only do so much so we should just focus on that."

She does have a challenge that most other entrepreneurs do not have – stingers! "I do

get stung occasionally if I'm not paying attention and my reactions are quite funny (think: cartoon balloon hand)." And like everyone starting in business, there are always a multitude of learning moments. "In the beginning, I wanted to test the virility of the seeds, so I spread what I thought was a normal amount of seeds into a small patch of garden. What I did not realize was that I had planted way too many seeds in one spot and there was actually someone's footprint in that exact spot. Several days later, I had wildflower seedlings growing in the perfect shape of a human foot," she shares with a laugh.

Chelsea is presently living in North Carolina but the Pollinator Project is still growing strong. Most recently, she collaborated with her sister Kelli Thoumsin, who is the owner of Bedhead Fiber, to produce a special seed packet. Bedhead Fiber

focuses in natural dyes and hand spun yarn, with an emphasis on foraging and sustainably harvesting natural products for their dyes. The sisters created a limited release seed packet specifically for dye flowers that are also a favorite for pollinators. Planting the seeds not only helps the bee populations but also produces flowers which can also be used to naturally dye textiles, reducing the impact of toxic chemicals on the environment.

Asked where she draws her strength and inspiration from, Chelsea simple says "Nature and the bees." She currently has three beehives and monitors them on a daily basis. "I now have a better understanding of their behavior in different weather, their patience and their dedication. I am convinced they know more than we do, and we need to respect that they know what they're doing."

Breakwater Vineyards
Jeanne and Bill Johnson

In Under the Tuscan Sun, author Frances Mayes writes, "Life offers you a thousand chances...all you have to do is take one." She might have been communicating directly to Jeanne and Bill Johnson with those words. In fact, they were in Tuscany, overlooking a beautiful vineyard when they reached a decision that would change their lives. Like the heroine in Mayes's novel, they wanted to live life more fully and had been looking for a business that they could start together. Looking out over the grapevines and Italian countryside that day, they decided that what they wanted to do was to start a vineyard.

Here however, their story diverges a little from that of the book. They choose to pursue their dream in the little town of Owls Head, Maine overlooking the Penobscot Bay. Not exactly the Italian countryside and a setting that inspires thoughts of lobsters, not wine. Nevertheless, the Johnson's were up for a challenge and in 2007, settled

"Life is a great adventure and you never know where it will lead you."

in to convert their recently purchased 32-acre horse farm into Breakwater Vineyards. They had complimentary business backgrounds and made a good team. "My background was in marketing and sales; Bill's was analytical," Jeanne explains. "The vineyard interested both of us – the chemistry in wine making caught Bill's attention, while I enjoyed networking and meeting people in our tasting room." However, with no direct experience in winemaking, let alone winemaking in a challenging climate like Maine, they knew that they would need some help.

Fortune favors the bold and that was the case with Bill and Jeanne as well. Just after they purchased their farm in Maine, a young winemaker from California contacted them about employment opportunities. He had just graduated from Fresno State University and, as his wife had grown up outside of Portland, was interested in moving to Maine. The Johnson's were still living in Massachusetts at the time and were in the early stages of creating a plan for their vineyard so they agreed to hire him as a consultant to help them get started. This winemaker – Brian Smith – could not have come on the scene at

a better time. Brian taught Bill and Jeane everything he could about growing grapes in a cold climate, making wine, sourcing grapes from other vineyards and guided their purchases of the equipment that they needed to get their business up and running.

The team's biggest challenge lay in trying to grow grapes in a climate that is not optimal. Their plan to tackle that was to utilize hardy varieties and to create hybrid grapes adapted for cold weather climates. They would also import grapes as needed to supplement what they were able to produce.

It sounds simple but converting a Maine horse farm into a vineyard is anything but easy. They started planting all of their grapevines by hand, digging over 3000 holes. The Johnson's had still not relocated, so they would arrive at their property on Friday night and work all day Saturday and Sunday digging holes and planting grapes. On Sunday nights, they would drive five hours back to Cape Cod to be ready to go to their full-time jobs again on Monday morning. "The grapevines didn't look like much those first few years and many old time Mainer's would just shake their heads and wave at us when we were out working in the vineyards," Jeanne recalls.

While they continued planting vines, converting the horse barn that would serve as their winery and purchasing equipment, Jeanne, Bill and Brian made plans regarding what they would focus on producing. They decided to start with four wines – an oaked Chardonnay, unoaked Chardonnay, Riesling and Pinot Noir. Why those varietals in particular? It was quite simple – Chardonnay is Jeanne's favorite, Brian liked Riesling and they knew that they would need a red wine so they decided on a Pinot Noir.

Jeanne's favorite vintage to date is their first oaked Chardonnay produced in 2010. "It was oaky and buttery just the way that I like it." They imported those grapes from Mudd Vineyards on Long Island and since whites need to be pressed immediately, they had to work with a grape processor while they were still sourcing their own equipment. According to Jeanne and Bill, still new to winemaking, "it was a great introduction to how wine is made and all the components that go into it beyond just grapes and yeast."

Starting out on a new journey is always fun and exciting and as the Johnson's slowly began to gain experience in their new profession, every day brought a unique twist and, to their way of thinking, more fun. Such was the case with their first vintage of Pinot Noir. "We bought those grapes from Hosmer Winery in the Finger Lakes," says Jeanne. "My husband and I rented a big truck and went out to Ovid, NY for the harvest. The only problem was that rain was forecast for our harvest day. It is not a good idea to harvest grapes in the rain as they absorb water. We did not bring any clothes and had not planned to stay over. Cameron Hosmer, the owner, suggested a

place to stay and loaned us his car so that we could get around without having to drive the truck. I remember seeing some of Hosmer's wines on a dinner menu and thought how cool that would be! We still have our Hosmer sweatshirts that we had to buy to get some clean clothes to wear the next day."

Slowly but surely, with the help of family and friends and a lot of hard work, Breakwater Vineyards began to take shape. The horse barn was converted to a winery that includes an Italian bottling line. The property now boasts 10 varieties of grapes including seven varieties of hybrids adapted for cold weather climates and they draw a lot of inspiration from their customers when determining what to produce next. "We started off with four dry wines and quickly realized that 50% of our visitors like sweet wines," recalls Jeanne.

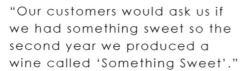

"Our customers would ask us if we had something sweet so the second year we produced a wine called 'Something Sweet'."

"We like to use local products whenever possible" explains Jeanne. "I have kept bees in the past and that is where we got the inspiration for our Bees Knees Mead. Our winemaker had never made a mead before so it was challenging to get the formula right."

Today, the winery uses several different types of grapes including Chardonnay, Pinot Noir, Riesling, Cayuga, Bianca, Prairie Star, Cabernet Sauvignon and Marquette. Some are still imported while others are cultivated in their own vineyards. They also use honey for their mead, apples for their hard apple cider and Maine blueberries for their Breakwater Blues Blueberry Wine, something that can be said to be uniquely Maine (and a big hit with visitors)!

Since, opening to the public in 2010, Breakwater Vineyards has continued to gain a steady local following as well as enticing visitors to the Maine Coast to visit their beautiful property overlooking the ocean. Thinking back to that rainy night in New York when she thought that it would be cool to see their wine on a menu, Jeanne says, "We are now distributed to over 300 locations in Maine and I was correct, it is pretty cool to see your wines on the wine list!"

"I think that our mead product is very special. It is made from local Maine honey. People have used it to toast special occasions like weddings. I am also a big fan of the honeybee and am amazed at how incredible they are. The mead has a nice backbone of appley acidity and just enough round sweetness to keep everything in delicate balance. Steam up some fresh Maine lobster and serve it with a chilled bottle of Bee's Knees and you'll think you've died and gone to heaven." - Jeanne

Long Ridge Farm
Poocham Hill Winery

Yarn: *Fingering Merino; Autumn's Mystery*
Natural, Autumn, Endangered, Art, Authentic

Wine: *2015 Frontenac*
New Hampshire, Deep Color, Cherry, Long Finish

Produced by college friends who ended up living less than a mile apart this pairing was destined to happen. The yarn is fine and soft, naturally dyed and produced by critically endangered sheep. The wine is aromatic and cheery with a fresh, inviting finish. Reflecting the people that make them, this pairing is friendly, warm and comfortable; just the thing to have on hand as you while away the hours on a neighbor's porch.

Long Ridge Farm
Nancy Zeller

Farming and wool are in Nancy Zeller's blood or at least they are passions that have been in her family for a long time. Her grandfather was a wool merchant in the early 1900s in Chicago and while genetics may not play a factor in it, Nancy is, by her own account "a total wool addict." "Once it gets cool in September, the wool comes out," she says happily. Her father was a farmer and Nancy grew up on a dairy farm in New Hampshire. These days, she is a shepherdess, natural dyer and the architect behind Umva, a natural textile-dyeing project in Rwanda.

"The key to succeeding is to try and have the nerve to fail."

After 28 years as a paralegal, Nancy and husband Jack (a retired police officer) relocated to Long Ridge Farm in Southwestern New Hampshire in what was for Nancy, a return to her rural roots. Nestled in the saddle of a ridge with Mount Manadnock to the east and the Connecticut River to the west, the place was calling out for some animals. In 2000, they purchased two Oxfords along with two additional fibery "mutt" sheep, put them together and created their first flock.

Not long after, she happened upon an article in *The Shepard* magazine which highlighted CVM/Romeldale sheep and was immediately fascinated with their breed and endangered status. Inspired by the thought that they could help preserve the species while at the same time producing some nice wool, Nancy reached out to Chris Spitzer who, at the time, was one of the largest breeders of CVM/Romeldale sheep in America. Considered critically endangered by The American Livestock Conservancy, these animals are an excellent choice for smaller farms because of their wonderful wool, hardiness and pleasant dispositions – just what Nancy was looking for. She sold her original four sheep and purchased a starter flock of a ram, ewe and two lambs, which arrived at Long Ridge Farm in 2002.

The sheep quickly made themselves at home and soon Jack and Nancy had a nice flock, happily munching away in the fields of their farm. The next task was to determine what to do with all of the fleece that they were soon getting. Nancy had taken up knitting but spinning was not something that interested her so for the first few years, they sold the fleece. Then, in 2005, she took a class in natural dyeing that changed her perspective on everything.

The natural dyeing class was like nothing that Nancy had ever experienced. The students went out, gathered ferns, flowers, and other things from nature, returned to the class, and worked outside over an open fire. When the yarns they were working with came out in the colors of nature, Nancy was amazed. She "knew of course that natural dyeing existed but had never experienced the results first hand. I raced home and immediately threw myself into it." She was soon studying with experts in the field and eventually connected with Earthues natural dye company and ended up as a distributor for them.

"It was an invigorating time," says Nancy. "I studied with a lot of well known natural dyers." She was experimenting with color creation and learning the complicated aspects of dyeing naturally. Long Ridge Farm was soon providing natural dyes so that customers could create their own colors as well as working to create custom colors, something that isn't always easy when you limit yourself to using natural products (Nancy never uses synthetic or chemical dyes). "One of my biggest challenges was the color gray. A customer brought in three pounds of fiber that she had spun from wool and bamboo and wanted it to be dyed a silver gray. I could make steel gray with no problem but as I started to try to create silver gray, I was not able to do it. Finally, frustrated, I tried 'phoning a friend' for help and reached out to a mentor. She honestly wanted me to figure it out on my own so I continued to experiment but after six months ended up sending the yarn back saying 'I just can't produce the color that you want.' I felt just awful having failed a customer – it was the worst thing that has even happened with my dyeing." Ultimately, Nancy discovered that she needed to incorporate another shade of gray from a dyestuff that she did not know about at the time and can now produce a silver gray color.

In addition to her obvious passion for dyeing, Nancy still produces wool from her sheep. She provides it as raw fleece and spinning fibers rather than having it made into yarn. "I want people to want and enjoy my wool and share in the creative process," she says.

One of Nancy's biggest projects developed in 2014 when she was working as a research resident in Rwanda, studying local plants and the colors that they could produce. She met a local family who was fascinated with her work and spent an afternoon with them experimenting with leaves and dyeing fabrics. The family loved it and so did Nancy. "I thought that this could be something," says Nancy. "The plants are here, the people want to learn and I have the experience and knowledge to bring it all together." The result was Umva, a project focused on the natural dyeing of fabrics using indigenous plants. The women involved in the project apply the dyes to fine wools and silks to create one of a kind pieces, which are sold through fair trade with the net proceeds returned to the families as income. This income brings empowerment, hope and freedom from poverty that in turn raises others up from poverty, causing a ripple effect that makes a difference for more Rwandans. Umva means 'listen' in Kinyarwanda, the language of Rwanda. Nancy, when asked where she draws her inspiration and creativity from, paused a moment and said "from the ability to be quiet and listen, relax, take in the world around me and think." If listening is the source of creation, it is the perfect name for a project that is allowing the women of Rwanda to create a better future for themselves and their families.

Reflecting back on her life, Nancy says "sometimes the path choses us and we can't image any other way – that is what happened to me. I can't imagine doing anything else." Looking into a crystal ball, she does not know what might be next but she "loves collaborating with others" and would like nothing better than seeing people from all around the world come together, have fun and create something artistically amazing (using only natural dyes of course)!

Poocham Hill Winery
Steve Robbins and Mame ODette

Located in southwestern New Hampshire, the seeds of Poocham Hill Winery were planted when owner Steve Robbins was eight years old and his parents gave him a chemistry set. He was enthralled and set to work on a variety of experiments. At twelve, he found a recipe for wine in a cookbook and went about creating it step by step as any good, young scientist would. As Steve recalls, "My parents encouraged me to do it, so I did. They thought the results were awful. My friends, on the other hand, thought the results were great. My dad took away my chemistry set after that!"

While his father may have taken away his tools, Steve had been infused with an interest in making wine. It was some time before he tried his hand at it again, but his interest and enthusiasm only grew as he got older. As a professional in the publishing industry, he traveled the world and always made time to try out new wines wherever he went.

With his wife Mame ODette, Steve finally returned to winemaking in the 1970s. They tried growing grapes in Keene, New Hampshire, "very unsuccessfully" says Mame. They had a bit more success several years later when Steve found a vineyard in Tilton, New Hampshire that had Marechal Foch wine grapes for sale. They drove their truck to the vineyard and spent the morning picking grapes. "When the truck was full and we had finished our lunch on that beautiful fall day, we headed home with enough fully ripened Marechal Foch grapes to make 20 gallons of wine," says Steve. "Our 1978 vintage of Marechal Foch was a success and was the start of our passion to grow our own wine grapes and produce excellent wine."

"Wine is something to be enjoyed."

A winery was not the only thing that they longed for however. When they first met, Steve had taught Mame to sail and they developed a love of boating together. Mame, who grew up on a farm, was also an avid gardener. Their life goals were to sail around the world and to buy a farm. Aiming to check the first one off their bucket list, they purchased a large sailboat and in 1991, set off to sail up and down the East Coast of the United States from Maine to the Caribbean. When the returned to dry land two years later, Mame said, "now how about that farm?"

With her background and passion for agriculture, Mame headed up the search and finally, in 1998, located a property that met her criteria. The one hundred and fifty acres had started out as a sheep farm and had fallen into a state of disrepair. It would be a lot of work but the couple felt that they would be up for the challenge. First, however, they needed to purchase the property. They were not the only ones interested and they found themselves bidding against a real estate investor who had plans to subdivide the property and build houses on it. Luckily for Steve and Mame, the owner loved the land as much as they did and wanted to see it preserved, so he ultimately sold it to them.

With the property obtained, they set about making it into a vegetable farm. Soon Poocham Hill Farm was producing organic vegetables for farmers markets and local co-ops in Brattleboro and Putney, Vermont. While Mame tended the vegetables, Steve, ever the wine enthusiast,

planted thirty Marechal Foch wine grape vines, recalling their earlier wine making success. He also started researching cold weather varietals and looking at the work of Minnesota viticulture pioneer Elmer Swenson who revolutionized grape growing in colder, short-seasoned regions through the creation of hybrids. The following year, Steve planted 140 vines and still more the year after that. Slowly and steadily, the hobby started to grow and become a business.

In 2004, the couple decided to convert the 1830s vintage barn on the property into a winery. The farming operation had also continued to grow and had become known for its garlic, fennel, heirloom tomatoes and leeks but in 2010, Mame decided to retire and work with Steve to make the winery into a successful business. Today, she focuses on using her growing expertise in the vineyards to produce

the highest quality wine grapes possible, while Steve is involved with the winemaking. Poocham Hill Winery has over 1,600 vines producing varietals such as Frontenac, Seyval, LaCrosse, St. Croix, Frontenac Gris, Marquette, Foch, Noiret and La Crescent.

Steve is passionate about producing New Hampshire wine using New Hampshire grapes and loves nothing more than convincing his visitors that good wine can be made in what wouldn't typically be thought of as 'wine-country.' One Sunday morning, a family visited Poocham Hill – a father and his 2 children. The gentleman tasted some of the wines that were being served and talked with Steve about his various vintages. He must have liked what he tasted because he ordered two cases on the spot, which for the small winery is an order that stands out. "I am the Secretary General for the Consulate of Peru at the United Nations," the man explained. "I want to show my neighbors in New York that they make real wine in New England." Steve had gained another convert!

Poocham comes from an Abenaki Indian word meaning "gathering place" and this part of the Connecticut River Valley

was a traditional meeting place for the native peoples. Today it remains largely rural but with the popularity of Poocham Hill Winery, more people are making the trek up the dirt road that leads to the farm every year. "In the summer, we get tourists from everywhere," says Steve. "We try to do it right and they seem to go away happy. It's a happy business."

Where do Steve and Mame want to go from here? They are largely satisfied with the size of their operation – just over the edge of a hobby and into a self-sustaining business. They are still learning; starting to make different blends from the grapes that they produce and receiving orders from appreciative customers all over the country. The future looks bright and they are pleased to be able to do what they are doing together on their beautiful farm in New Hampshire. "It's magical," says Steve looking out the window. "I love this place."

Fun Fact:
While working in publishing, Steve was on the team which created, wrote and named the first '...For Dummies' book.

The Patterns

Cornhill Shawl
Victoria Magnus, Eden Cottage Yarns

This is a simple but pretty and practical shawl, designed to be relaxing and easy enough for travel - and TV knitting. It requires no counting, no stitch markers, and no purling. It's designed to use approximately 400m of each of two colours of 4ply yarn.

Materials
Eden Cottage Yarns Milburn 4ply (4ply/fingering; 85% (Superwash Bluefaced Leicester); 200m/218yds per 50g skein)

MC: Natural; 2 x 50g balls

CC: Harvest Gold; 2 x 50g balls

Note: This shawl is designed to use approximately 400m per colour, however if you have a little more or a little less, simply work to where you want to, stop, and jump to 'final row' section, making sure you have enough to work that plus a stretchy enough cast off.

Ideally, work that row plus the cast off in the opposite colour to that which you were just working with.

Needles and Accessories
One 3.5mm (US 4) circular needle, 80cm (32in) length (or the size needed to obtain the correct gauge).

If you prefer more space for stitches on your cable you may find it easier to work with a 100-150cm (40-60in) circular needle.

Size
194 cm (76.3 in) wingspan x 35 cm (13.7 in) depth, blocked.

Gauge
17sts and 48 rows to 10cm (4in) over garter stitch on 3.5mm (US 4) needles after blocking.

Abbreviations
CC	Contrast colour
k2tog	Knit two together
k	Knit
kfb	Knit into the front of the stitch, leave it on the left needle and knit again but into the back loop (increases 1 stitch)
MC	Main colour
Rep	Repeat
RS	Right side
Sts	Stitches
WS	Wrong side
yo	Yarn over

Pattern Notes
To create a stretchy edge knit the first stitch of each row twice as follows: k1, place that stitch back on left-hand needle and k1 again.

Pattern
Using MC cast on 6.

Garter section (in MC)
Row 1 (RS): k1, kfb, yo, k to last 2 sts, kfb, k1. 9 sts
Row 2 (WS): k1, kfb, yo, k to last 2 sts, kfb, k1. 12 sts
Rep rows 1 - 2 a further five times. 42 sts

Stripe section
Using CC
Row 13 (RS): k1, kfb, yo, k to last 2 sts, kfb, k1. 45 sts
Row 14 (WS): k1, kfb, yo, k to last 2 sts, kfb, k1. 48 sts

Using MC
Row 15 (RS): k1, kfb, yo, k to last 2 sts, kfb, k1. 51 sts
Row 16 (WS): k1, kfb, yo, k to last 2 sts, kfb, k1. 54 sts
Rep the last four rows (two stripes) a further two
times. 78 sts

Lace section
Using CC
Row 25 (RS): k1, kfb, yo, k to last 2 sts, kfb, k1. 81 sts
Row 26 (WS): k1, kfb, yo, k to last 2 sts, kfb, k1. 84 sts
Rep rows 25 and 26 a further two times. 96 sts.
Row 31 (RS): k1, kfb, yo, k1, *yo, k2tog* rep to
last 3 sts, k1, kfb, k1. 99 sts
Row 32 (WS): k1, kfb, yo, k to last 2 sts, kfb, k1.
102 sts

Rep rows 25 and 26 a further two times. 114 sts

Rep Garter Section, Stripe Section and Lace Section
a further three times.

Stitch count at the end of each rep should be 222
sts, 330 sts, and 438 sts.

Fifth rep - work Garter Section and Stripe Section
(510 sts), then work End Section.

End Section
Using CC
*(Having worked the previous row in MC. If your
previous row was in CC then reverse colours for this
section).*

Next row (RS): k1, kfb, yo, k to last 2 sts, kfb, k1.
513 sts
Next row (WS): k1, kfb, yo, k to last 2 sts, kfb, k1.
516 sts

Using MC
Cast off loosely, using a larger needle size if
necessary.

Give the cast off edging a tug as you go along
to make sure the stitches are coming out loose
enough.

Finishing
Weave in ends and block gently into a shallow
crecent/banana shape.

Garter stitch benefits from being blocked gently in
order to create a cozy fabric so we recommend not
stretching the shawl downwards too much.

Spring in the Meadow
Susan Rice, Bartlettyarns, Inc.

Supplies Needed:

Size 7 Single Pointed Needles
Yarn Needle
5 skeins yarn - wild grape, wheat, raspberry, black, white
are shown in photo

Instructions:

Cast on 84 stiches and knit 5 rows in Wild Grape ending
with a right side row.

With Wheat purl next two rows. With Wild Grape, knit
5 rows ending with a right side row. This is a total of 12
rows.

Follow chart pattern in stockinette stich (knit right side
row, purl wrong side row), changing colors as indicated.

When finished with the chart pattern on the reverse,
switch to wheat and knit 5 rows and bind off.

To cover the back side of the sheep, where you have
carried yarn from one sheep to the next, cast on 84
stitches and knit a band of 25 rows, bind off. Sew into
place.

Final finishing: Pick up stiches evenly along the edge
and knit 5 rows.

Bind off, fold over and stich into place on wrong side.

Note: You will have a double layer to pick up stiches
thru in place where the band is located.

Wash and Block to shape. Cool water is recommended
and a few drops of dish washing soap. Rinse with same
temp cool water, loosly wringing dry and lie flat to dry.

CHART NOTE: Pattern is read left to right on right
side rows and right to left on wrong side rows,
starting at the bottom of the chart.

Sheep body is done in Winter White. Sheep face
and legs are done in Black.

Purple = Wild Grape. Pink = Raspberry. Yellow =
Wheat

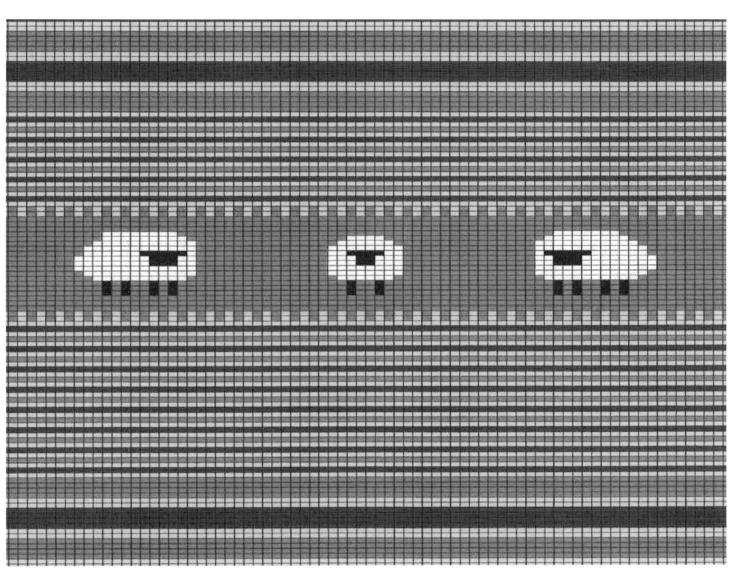

Strike up the Bands
Randy Glick, Pik Ka Handbag

The basic concept of knitting on the bias – or diagonal – gives you a finished piece that holds its shape better and provides added stretch. You achieve knitting on the bias by increasing at the beginning of each row – Knit 1 Front and Back (K1FB). By bringing your yarn to the front of your work and slipping the last stitch purl-wise you have the perfect "anchor" for attaching ribbing, a fancy edging, or even a thumb.

All of the patterns have some similar components that, once you master them, will become second nature. I call them "The Point" – how you start each piece; "The Turn" – how you turn the first corner; and, "The Other Turn" – how you finish off a piece. Numbers are provided to make small/medium/large sizes. You will need size 6, 16 inch cable and a set of size 6 double pointed needles (DPN) for all patterns.

The Point
Knit cast on (CO) 3 stitches
Row 1: Purl 1 (P1), Knit 1 Front and Back (K1FB), with yarn in front (WYIF) Slip 1 Purlwise (SI1P) (4 Stitches)
Row 2: Knit 1 (K1), K1FB, K1, WYIF SI1P (5 Stitches)
Row 3 (Pattern Row): K1, K1FB, [Slip 1 Knitwise (SI1K), K1], WYIF SI1P (6 Stitches)
Row 4: K1, K1FB, knit to last stitch, WYIF SI1P (7 stitches)
Row 5 (And all odd numbered rows): K1, K1FB, [SL1K, K1], WYIF SI1P
Repeat Rows 4 & 5 until the piece is the desired width

HELPFUL HINT: Until you get used to the "look," Pattern Rows are done when you have an odd number of stitches (Row 5) on your needle and "knit rows" when you have an even number of stitches (Row 4). If your Pattern Row was done correctly the second to last stitch is a knit stitch.

The Turn – (Done on a knit row)
Row 1: K3, turn work
Row 2: K2, WYIF SI1P
Row 3: K1, K2TOG, knit to last stitch, WYIF SI1P
Row 4: K1, K1FB, [SL1K, K1], WYIF SI1P
Repeat Rows 3 & 4 until the piece is the desired length on the longest side.

The Other Turn - (Done on a purl row)
Row 1: K3, turn work
Row 2: K2, WYIF SI1P
Row 3: K1, K2TOG, K1, [SL1K, K1], WYIF SI1P
Row 4: K1, K2TOG, knit to last stitch, WYIF SI1P
Repeat Rows 3 & 4 until you have 7 stitches left.
Row 1: K1, K2TOG, K1, SL1K, K1, WYIF SI1P (6 stitches)
Row 2: K1, K2TOG, K2, WYIF SI1P (5 stitches)
Row 3: K1, K2TOG, K1, WYIF SI1P (4 stitches) through loop
Row 4: K1, K2TOG, BO 1st stitch, K1, BO 2nd stitch, cut yarn, draw through loop

The Scarf
The scarf is essentially a long band. You can decide if you want a long narrow scarf, or something wider. Materials: 300-400 yards of "painted" yarn

Follow pattern for "The Point," knit until desired width, follow pattern for "The Turn," knit until desired length (I recommend at least 6 feet), follow pattern for "The Other Turn." Weave in all loose ends. Wash and block.

The Headband
The headband is a narrower band with a rolled ribbing attached to the two long edges. Materials: 200 yards "painted" yarn.

Follow pattern for "The Point," knit until you have 22 stitches on needle, follow pattern for "The Turn," knit until desired length (20/22/24 inches), follow pattern for "The Other Turn."

Remember – the rolled ribbing will add about 1 inch to the width.

Rolled Ribbing

TOP - Pick up front loop of stitches created by the "WYIF SI1P." (see diagram) Join and knit 10 rounds. Roll ribbing back and join with back loop of stitches created by the "WYIF SI1P" by K2TOG (one live stitch and one of the back stitches), binding off as you go along. Cut yarn. Cut yarn of enough length to attach the two short edges closing the opening at the back.

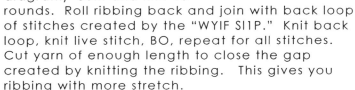

BOTTOM - Pick up front loop of stitches created by the "WYIF SI1P." (see diagram) Join and knit 10 rounds. Roll ribbing back and join with back loop of stitches created by the "WYIF SI1P." Knit back loop, knit live stitch, BO, repeat for all stitches. Cut yarn of enough length to close the gap created by knitting the ribbing. This gives you ribbing with more stretch.

The Hat

Materials: 250-300 yards of "painted" yarn

Follow pattern for "The Point," knit until you have 22 stitches on needle, follow pattern for "The Turn," knit until desired length (20/22/24 inches), follow pattern for "The Other Turn." Remember – the rolled ribbing will add about 1 inch to the width.

Follow pattern for "Rolled Ribbing - BOTTOM."

Be sure to leave long tails, these will be used to sew the edge openings around the inset thumb closed.

For the crown of the hat, pick up front loop of stitches created by the "WYIF SI1P." (see diagram). Join and knit 10 rounds. Roll ribbing back and join with back loop of stitches created

by the "WYIF SI1P" by K2TOG (one live stitch and one of the back stitches). DO NOT bind off as you go along. Knit 9/12/15 rounds.

Divide stitches evenly on three double pointed needles. Decreases are worked on the first and last three stitches of each needle, a total of six decreases on each round.

Row 1: [K1, K2TOG, knit to last three stitches, Slip Slip Knit (SSK), K1] three times

Row 2: Knit

Repeat Row 1 &2 until you have 4 stitches left on each needle, K2TOG around, cut yarn and with a darning needle pull the cut end through the remaining 6 stitches. Draw tightly and weave in end.

Whip stitch opening closed. Weave in any remaining ends, being careful to close any gaps remaining from the rolled ribbing.

Bubbles
Jeane deCoster, Elemental Affects

Yarn: Elemental Affects Shetland Fingering yarn, 1 skein each of a light, medium and dark shade. As knit: Color A = Black; Color B = Emsket (grey); Color C = Sea Foam

Notions: Stitch markers and US size 2 double point needles. Short stitch holders (2) (Optional: US Size 2 short glove needles for thumb.)

Fingerless mittens worked from cuff to knuckles. Makes 2.

Cuff
With Color A and stretchy type cast on – cast on 108 stitches; join in the round and place a marker to indicate beginning of row (BOR).

Round 1: *K2tog, p2tog; repeat from * to end.
Rounds 2 - 4: *K1, p1; repeat from * to end.

Start next Round with first row of Chart A (Corrugated Rib)– change colors as indicated on chart(s) – repeating stitches 1 and 2 around Cuff.

Repeat rows 2 – 5 a total of 3 times. Repeat rows 2 – 5 once more. 16 rounds of Corrugated Rib.

Hand
Rounds 1: With Color B, knit entire round – increasing 6 stitches evenly around cuff – 60 sts total.

Rounds 2 and 3: With Color B, knit. On Round 3, place Marker (PM) before and after first stitch to separate the base of the Thumb.

Start next Round with Row 1, Stitch 1 of Chart B (Hand) and end with first row of Chart C – Thumb. (Slip markers before first yo and after last yo of Thumb stitches.)

Work all 9 rows of Chart B (hand) twice and rows 1 – 3 a third time while working all rows of Chart C – Thumb once.

Put Thumb on hold to complete Hand.

Next Round: Put the 20 Thumb stitches on one or more small stitch holders and continue with row 4 of Chart B only. At the end of the round using a Thumb Wrap cast on method – cast on 13 stitches in pattern and replace BOR marker.

Next Round: Continue with rows 5 – 9 and rows 1 – 3 of Chart B.

Next Rounds: Work rows 2 – 5 of Chart A.

Next 3 Rounds: With Color A, *k1, p1; repeat from * to end of round.

With Color A, bind off all stitches using a stretchy bind off technique.

Finish Thumb
Transfer 10 thumb stitches to first glove needle, remaining 10 thumb stitches to second glove needle. With third glove needle, pick up 12 more thumb stitches at the base of the thumb – placing a marker between 6 and 7 of these new stitches – BOR for the thumb.

Next Rounds: Starting with Color B, k2togB, k1C, k2togB, K2togC, (k1B, k1C) 9 times, k2togC, k2togB, k1C, k2togB; 26 stitches remaining.

Next 4 Rounds: Work rows 2 – 5 of Chart A.

Next 3 Rounds: With Color A, *k1, p1; repeat from * to end of round.

With Color A, bind off all stitches using a stretchy bind off technique.

Turn mitten inside out. With tapestry needle, weave in all ends.

Wet finish by squeezing firmly in hot soapy water 20 or 30 times; repeat in cool clear water until soap has been removed. Pat into shape to dry on a towel. If necessary, press lightly with steam iron.

Chart A - Cuff
(Corrugated Rib)
Stitch Repeat - 2 stitches

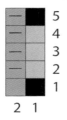

Chart B - Hand
(Bubbles Pattern)

Stitch Repeat - 8 stitches + 5 to center

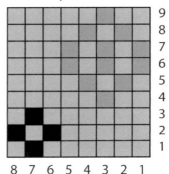

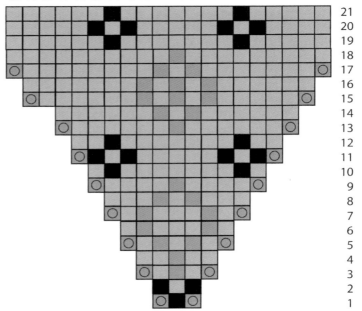

The Recipes

Oven-Browned Sole with Asparagus

Wine: Peyton Paige Sauvignon Blanc
Winery: McGrail Vineyards

Prep and Cook Time: 15 Mins
Servings: Approx. 4

Ingredients
* 1 1/2 pounds asparagus (1/2 in. thick)
* 1 pound boned, skinned sole fillets (1/4 in. thick)
* 1/4 cup all-purpose flour
* 1/2 teaspoon salt
* 1/2 teaspoon pepper
* 1/2 cup butter
* 1 cup dry white wine such as Sauvignon Blanc
* 3 tablespoons coarsely chopped fresh tarragon

Directions
* Rinse and drain asparagus. Snap off and discard ends.
* Rinse fish and pat dry.
* In a plastic bag, combine flour, salt, and pepper.
* Shake 1 or 2 pieces of fish at a time in flour mixture to coat, shaking off excess as you remove the fillets from bag. Discard leftover flour mixture.
* Put 2 tablespoon butter in a 10- by 15-inch baking pan and 3 tablespoons butter in another 10- by 15-inch pan.
* Set pans in a 500°F oven until butter is melted, 1 to 2 minutes.
* Place asparagus in pan with smaller amount of butter; turn to coat spears.
* Place fish in remaining pan; turn to coat in butter and lay in a single layer.
* Return pans to oven and roast until asparagus is tender-crisp to bite and fish is opaque but still moist-looking in center of thickest part (cut to test), approximately 4 to 5 minutes.
* Transfer asparagus and fish to a platter and keep warm.
* Pour wine into fish-roasting pan and add 3 tablespoons tarragon. Set pan over two burners on high heat and bring to a boil.
* Stir until wine is reduced to 1/3 cup, about 2 minutes.
* Remove from heat and stir in remaining butter until blended.
* Pour sauce into a bowl.
* Scatter remaining 1/2 tablespoon tarragon over fish. Serve fish and asparagus with sauce - add to taste.

Chocolate Cupcakes with Chocolate Buttercream

Wine: 2014 Rolling Hills
Winery: Black Ankle Vineyards

Prep and Cook time: 55 min
Servings: Approx. 15

Ingredients

For Chocolate Cupcakes:
* 1 cup all-purpose flour
* 1 cup sugar
* 1/3 cup cocoa powder
* 1 teaspoon baking soda
* 1/2 teaspoon baking powder
* 1/2 teaspoon salt
* 1 large egg
* 1/2 cup buttermilk
* 1/4 cup vegetable oil
* 1 1/2 teaspoons pure vanilla extract

For Frosting:
* 1 cup (2 sticks) unsalted butter
* 2-3 cups confectioners' sugar, sifted
* 3/4 - 1 cup unsweetened cocoa powder
* 2 teaspoons pure vanilla extract
* Dash of salt
* 2-3 tablespoons heavy cream

Directions

For Chocolate Cupcakes:
* Preheat oven to 350°F. Line muffin tins with cupcake liners.
* Sift together all the dry ingredients in a bowl
* In separate bowl, combine all the wet ingredients using a whisk.
* Mix the dry ingredients using mixer at low speed for 1 minute. Add the wet ingredients. Mix for 3 minutes on medium speed.
* Divide evenly among the cupcake liners.
* Bake for 12-15 minutes checking with a toothpick.
* Cool cupcakes completely.

For Chocolate Frosting:
- Whip butter with electric mixer on medium speed for about 2-3 minutes (should be light and creamy when finished). Add the powdered sugar, cocoa powder, vanilla and salt and mix until combined. Increase speed to medium-high and whip for 2-3 minutes.
- Add heavy cream and beat on medium-high for an additional minute or two.
- Frost cupcakes and decorate as desired

Vegetarian Tostadas

Wine: Bees Knees Mead
Winery: Breakwater Vineyards

Servings: Approx. 6

Ingredients
- 2 teaspoons olive oil
- 1 cup onion, diced small
- 2 cloves garlic, minced
- 1 cup red potatoes, diced small
- 1 cup Sweet potatoes, diced small
- 1 cup zucchini, diced small
- 1 15 oz. can black beans
- 1 cup frozen sweet corn
- 1-2 tablespoons chili powder
- 2 teaspoons oregano
- 2 teaspoons basil
- 1 teaspoon salt
- 1/2 cup water
- 6 whole wheat flour tortillas
- Cooking spray
- Guacamole
- Salsa
- Sour cream
- Shredded Cheddar cheese, Colby cheese and Monterey Jack
- Fresh cilantro

Directions
- Preheat oven to 350°F.
- Spray flour tortillas with cooking spray.
- Bake in oven until crisp and brown.
- Heat sauté pan to medium heat and add olive oil.
- When hot, add onions, and garlic. Sauté approx. 5 minutes then add remaining vegetables except black beans and corn.
- Sauté another 5 minutes then add seasonings.
- Sauté 1 additional minute and add water.
- Simmer mixture until potatoes are tender.
- Stir in beans and corn, heat until all ingredients are hot and water is evaporated.
- Serve on toasted flour tortillas and garnish with guacamole, salsa, sour cream, shredded cheeses, and cilantro

Chicken Enchiladas

Wine: 2015 Alpenglo Riesling
Winery: Colorado Cellars

Servings: Approx. 8

Ingredients
- 8 (6-inch) corn tortillas
- Cooking spray
- 1 tablespoon chopped onion
- 1 tablespoon chopped fresh cilantro
- 3 cups shredded cooked chicken breast
- 3 (10-ounce) cans enchilada sauce, divided
- 1 1/2 cups (6 ounces) shredded reduced-fat sharp Cheddar cheese
- 1/2 cup diced tomato
- 4 cups shredded iceberg lettuce

Directions
- Preheat oven to 350°F.
- Wrap tortillas in aluminum foil; bake at 350°F for 15 minutes.
- While tortillas are baking, coat a large nonstick skillet with cooking spray; place over medium-high heat until hot. Add onion, cilantro; sauté until onion is tender. Add chicken and 1 can enchilada sauce; cook 5 minutes.
- Spoon chicken mixture evenly down centers of tortillas. Roll up tortillas; place, seam sides down, in a 13- x 9-inch baking dish. Heat remaining 2 cans enchilada sauce in a saucepan; pour over enchiladas, and top with cheese. Bake at 350°F for 10 minutes or until enchiladas are thoroughly heated and cheese melts. Sprinkle evenly with tomato. Serve over lettuce.

Watermelon and Arugula Salad

Wine: 2016 Hensell Rosé
Winery: Kuhlman Cellars

Ingredients
- 3 tablespoons extra-virgin olive oil
- 1 tablespoon freshly squeezed lemon juice
- 1 teaspoon honey
- Salt
- Pepper
- 6 cups baby arugula
- 3 cups diced seedless watermelon
- 1/2 cup goat cheese
- 1/3 cup smoked bacon

Directions
- In a small bowl, whisk together the olive oil, lemon juice, honey and shallot
- Season to taste with salt and pepper
- Optional: You can add more lemon juice or honey to make the vinaigrette more tart or sweet if you prefer.
- In a large serving bowl, combine the arugula and watermelon.
- Add the vinaigrette and toss to combine.
- Sprinkle the salad with the goat cheese and bacon or serve alongside so that guests may add to their own taste or as a vegetarian option

Gingerbread Squares with Whipped Cream

Wine: Glögg
Winery: HETTA

Ingredients

For Gingerbread:
- 8-1/4 oz. (1-3/4 cups plus 2 Tbs.) flour
- 1-1/2 teaspoons baking soda
- 2-1/4 teaspoons ground ginger
- 1/2 teaspoon ground cinnamon
- 1/4 teaspoon ground cloves
- Pinch salt
- 2-1/2 oz. (5 tablespoons) butter, softened at room temperature
- 1/3 cup sugar
- 1 large egg
- 3/4 cup dark molasses
- 3/4 cup cold water

For Whipped Cream:
- 1 cup heavy cream
- 1/4 cup maple syrup

Directions
- Heat the oven to 350°F. Butter an 9×9-inch cake pan.
- Sift together the flour, baking soda, ginger, cinnamon, cloves, and salt onto a sheet of waxed paper. Set aside.
- In a large mixing bowl, beat the butter until light and creamy.
- Add the sugar and continue beating until light and fluffy.
- Add the egg and beat until well combined. Scrape down the sides of the bowl and pour in the molasses in a slow, steady stream, beating all the while.
- Add half of the sifted dry ingredients and mix just until well combined.
- Mix in the remaining dry ingredients. Slowly pour in the coldwater and stir until well incorporated.
- Pour the batter into the prepared pan and bake 35 to 40 minutes (testing with toothpick)
- Let cool in the pan about 1 hour before serving.
- Beat the cream until thickened. Slowly pour in the syrup and continue beating until the cream holds soft peaks.
- Cut the cake into squares; serve with the whipped cream.

Slow-Cooker Pulled Pork with BBQ Sauce

Wine: 2015 Mother Clone Zinfandel
Winery: Pedroncelli Winery

Ingredients

For Pork:
- 1 (6-7 pound) boneless Boston butt, cut in half (shoulder roast)
- Salt
- Pepper

For Sauce:
- 2 (28 oz) cans crushed tomatoes
- 12 ounces molasses
- 2 small onions, peeled and cut
- 1/2 cup organge juice
- 2 tablespoons Worcestershire sauce
- 2-4 chipotle chilies in adobo sauce, chopped (add as many as you would like)
- 2 cloves garlic, peeled and crushed
- 2 teaspoons ground allspice
- Salt
- Black Pepper

Directions

For Sauce:
- In a 6-quart saucepan, combine the tomatoes, molasses, onion, orange juice, Worcestershire sauce, chipotles, garlic, and all-spice. Add salt and pepper to taste.
- Bring to a simmer over medium-high heat.
- Reduce the heat to low and cook, uncovered, stirring occasionally, for 30 minutes.
- Use the immersion blender to mix the ingredients into a smooth sauce. (Or transfer to the stand blender and puree for about 60 seconds.)
- Simmer, stirring frequently, for an additional 45 minutes or until the sauce is reduced to about 2 quarts.

For Pork:
- Rub the meat with salt and pepper and put it in the slow cooker. 6 cups of the barbecue sauce, then cover and cook on high for 7 to 8 hours or on low for 10 to 11 hours.
- The meat should be fork-tender and falling apart.
- Remove the meat and place in a large bowl to cool.
- After the cooking liquid has sat for a few minutes, strain the fat.
- When the meat is cool enough, shred it with your fingers, pulling off the remaining fat and gristle.

- Toss 2 to 3 cups of the cooking sauce with the meat, and add more as needed to keep it moist.

Serve on buns and pour the reserved sauce on top.

Melon and Prosciutto Salad with Parmigiano-Reggiano

Wine: 2016 Pinot Noir Rosé
Winery: Elk Cove Vineyards

Servings: Approx. 8

Ingredients
- 3 cups cubed honeydew melon – small cubes (about 1/2 melon)
- 3 cups cubed cantaloupe – small cubes (about 1 melon)
- 2 tablespoons sliced fresh mint
- 1 teaspoon fresh lemon juice
- 1/4 teaspoon freshly ground black pepper
- 2 ounces thinly sliced prosciutto, cut into thin strips
- 3/4 cup shaved fresh Parmigiana-Reggiano cheese

Directions
- Combine first 5 ingredients, tossing gently.
- Arrange melon mixture on a serving platter.
- Arrange prosciutto evenly over melon mixture.
- Sprinkle with Parmigiana-Reggiano.

Carolina Rolled Pork

Wine: 2015 Frontenac
Winery: Poocham Hill Winery

Prep and Cook Time: 30 min
Servings: Aprox. 6-8

Ingredients
- 1 pound sliced bacon
- 1 ½ pound pork tenderloin
- 1 ½ cup barbecue sauce (mustard-based or other)
- Salt and black pepper to taste

Directions
- Preheat a grill for medium heat. When hot, lightly oil the grate.
- While the grill is heating, slice the pork tenderloin into flat

strips similar to the bacon.
- Roll up strips of bacon inside strips of pork tenderloin and secure with moistened toothpicks.
- Season with salt and pepper.
- Grill the rolls for about 10 minutes on one side, then turn over.
- Spread barbecue sauce over them and cook for another 10 minutes.
- Remove from the grill and let rest for 2 minutes before serving.

Italian Chopped Salad in Shells

Wine: 2014 Old Vine Zinfandel
Winery: Dry Creek Vineyard

Ingredients
- 1 (16 ounce) package jumbo pasta shells
- 4 cups chopped romaine lettuce
- 1/2 cup chopped fresh basil
- 1 cup coarsely chopped cooked chicken
- 3/4 cup coarsely chopped tomatoes
- 3/4 cup coarsely chopped cucumber
- 3 ounces salami, chopped
- 1 cup parmesan cheese
- bacon vinaigrette dressing
- 2 tablespoons red wine vinegar
- 2 teaspoons Dijon mustard
- 2 slices, crumbled cooked bacon
- ½ teaspoon salt
- Black pepper (to taste)
- ½ cup olive oil

Directions
- Cook pasta shells as directed on the package. Drain and cool.
- Place remaining ingredients except vinaigrette in a medium bowl.
- Prepare vinaigrette dressing:
  * Whisk red wine vinegar, Dijon mustard and salt.
  * Add black pepper to taste.
  * Add bacon
  * Gradually whisk in olive oil
- Pour vinaigrette over the salad, toss to coat.
- Stuff the shells with the salad.
- Cover and refrigerate 2 hours before serving.

Caramel Filled Chocolate Cookies

Wine: 2016 Golubok
Winery: Olalla Vineyard and Winery

Prep and Cook Time: 30 minutes
Servings: Approx. 24

Ingredients
- 1 cup butter, softened
- 1 cup white sugar
- 1 cup packed brown sugar
- 2 eggs
- 2 teaspoons vanilla extract
- 2 1/4 cups all-purpose flour
- 1 teaspoon baking soda
- 3/4 cup unsweetened cocoa powder
- 1 tablespoon white sugar
- 48 chocolate-covered caramel candies

Directions
- Beat butter until creamy.
- Gradually beat in white sugar and brown sugar.
- Beat in eggs and vanilla.
- Combine flour, baking soda, and cocoa. Gradually add to butter mixture, beating well.
- Cover and chill at least 2 hours.
- Preheat oven to 375°F.
- Place 1 tablespoon sugar into small bowl
- Divide the dough into 4 parts. Work with one part at a time, leaving the remainder in the refrigerator until needed.
- Divide each part into 12 pieces.
- Quickly press each piece of dough around a chocolate covered caramel.
- Roll into a ball.
- Dip the tops into the sugar.
- Place sugar side up, 2 inches apart on greased baking sheets.
- Bake for 8 minutes in the preheated oven.
- Let cool for 3 to 4 minutes on the baking sheets before removing to wire racks to finish cooling.

Designers

Laura Aylor
"Faberge"
laylor13@gmail.com
Facebook: Fogbound Knits
Instagram: lauraaulow
Twitter: LAylor13
Ravelry: LauraAylor
"Faberge" pattern: www.ravelry.com/patterns/library/faberge

Michele Brown
"Great Divide Shawl"
www.republicofwool.com
Facebook: RepublicWool
Instagram: republicofwool
Ravelry: kisskisskido
"Great Divide Shawl" pattern: http://www.ravelry.com/patterns/library/great-divide-shawl

Jeane deCoster
"Bubbles"
Elemental Affects
jeanedecoster@elementalaffects.com
Instagram: elemental-affects
Ravelry: decostj

Randy Glick
"Strike Up the Bands"
Pik Ka Handbag
pikkahandbag@outlook.com
www.pik-ka-handbag.com
Instagram: pik_ka_handbag

Keya Kuhn
"Cygnus Lace Shawl"
Cedar Hill Farm Company
cedarhillyarns@gmail.com
www.cedarhillfarmcompany.com
Facebook: cerdarhillfarmcompany
Instagram: cerdarhillyarns
Twitter: cedarhillfarmco
Pinterest: Cedar Hill Farm Company
Ravelry: Zibelineknits

Victoria Magnus
"Cornhill Shawl"
Eden Cottage Yarns
edencottageyarns@gmail.com
www.edencottageyarns.co.uk
Facebook: Eden-Cottage-Yarns
Instagram: EdenCottageYarns
Twitter: edencottage
Ravelry: vmagnus
"Cornhill Shawl" pattern: http://www.ravelry.com/patterns/library/cornhill

Lisa Mutch
"Thrice"
northboundknitting.etsy.com
www.northboundknitting.com
Facebook: northbound knitting
Instagram: nbknitting
Twitter: nbknitting
Ravelry: nbknitting
"Thrice" pattern: http://www.ravelry.com/patterns/library/thrice

Ambah O'Brien
"Miso"
www.ambah.co
Facebook: ambahknitdesign
Instagram: ambahobrien
Ravelry: ambahobrien
"Miso" pattern: http://www.ravelry.com/patterns/library/miso

Paulina Popiolek
"Meadow"
Paulina.popiolek@yahoo.co.uk
Instagram: paulina.popiolek
Ravelry: paulinap
"Meadow" pattern: www.ravelry.com/patterns/library/meadow-14

Susan Rice
"Spring in the Meadow"
Barlettyarns Inc.
sales@bartlettyarn.com
www.bartlettyarns.com
Facebook: Bartlettyarns
Instagram: Bartlettyarns
Ravelry: bartlettyarns

Cynthia Spencer
"Quick Knit Hat"
www.reallyclear.com
Facebook: reallyclear
Instagram: reallyclear
Ravelry: ReallyClear
"Quick Knit Hat" pattern: http://www.ravelry.com/patterns/library/quick-knit-hat

Wineries

Black Ankle Vineyards
14463 Black Ankle Rd.
Mt. Airy, MD
(301) 829-3338
info@blackankle.com
www.blackankle.com
Facebook: blackanklevineyards
Instagram: blackanklevineyards
Twitter: blackanklevines

Breakwater Vineyards
35 Ash Point Dr.
Owls Head, ME
(207) 595-1721
info@breakwatervineyards.com
www.breakwatervineyards.com
Facebook: Breakwater Vineyards

Colorado Cellars
3553 E Rd.
Palisade, CO
(970) 464-7921
info@coloradocellars.com
www.coloradocellars.com

Dry Creek Vinyard
3770 Lambert Bridge Road
Healdsburg, CA
(707) 433-1000
dcv@drycreekvineyard.com
www.drycreekvineyard.com
Facebook: drycreekvineyard
Instagram: drycreekvineyard
Twitter: DryCreekVnyd

Elk Cove Vineyards
27751 NW Olson Rd.
Gaston, OR
(503) 985-7760
info@elkcove.com
www.elkcove.com
Facebook: elkcove
Instagram: elkcove
Twitter: elkcove

Kuhlman Cellars
18421 E US Hwy 290
Stonewall, TX
(512) 920-2675
appointments@kuhlmancellars.com
www.kuhlmancellars.com
Facebook: kuhlmancellars
Twitter: KuhlmanCellars

HETTA Glögg
PO Box 605
Rhinebeck, NY
(845) 216-4801
darren@hettaglogg.com
www.hettaglogg.com
Facebook: hettaglogg
Instagram: hettaglogg

McGrail Vineyards and Winery
5600 Greenville Rd.
Livermore, CA
(925) 215-0717
info@mcgrailvineyards.com
www.mcgrailvineyards.com
Facebook: LivermoreWine
Instagram: mcgrail_vineyards
Twitter: McGrailVineyard

NorthLeaf Winery
232 S Janesville St.
Milton, WI
(608) 580-0575
info@northleafwinery.com
www.northleafwinery.com
Instagram: northleafwinery

Olalla Vineyard and Winery
13176 Olalla Valley Rd. SE
Olalla, WA
(253) 851-4949
www.olallawines.com
Facebook: olallawines
Twitter: WinesOlalla

Pedroncelli Winery
1220 Canyon Rd.
Geyserville, CA
(707) 857-3531
Service@pedroncelli.com
www.pedroncelli.com
Facebook: PedroncelliWinery
Instagram: pedroncelliwine
Twitter: pedroncelli

Poocham Hill Winery and Vineyards
226 Poocham Road
Westmoreland, NH
(603) 399-4496
poochamwinery@gmail.com
www.poochamwinery.com

Dyers and Yarn

Baa Baa Brighouse
11 Church Street
Rastrick, Brighouse
West Yorkshire, United Kingdom
01484 722662
info@baabaabrighouse.co.uk
www.baabaabrighouse.co.uk
Facebook: BaaBaaBrighouse
Instagram: baabaabrighouse
Twitter: BaaBaaBrighouse
Ravelry: baa-baa-brighouse

Bartlettyarns Inc.
20 Water Street
Harmony, ME
sales@bartlettyarns.com
www.bartlettyarns.com
Facebook: Bartlettyarns
Instagram: Bartlettyarns
Ravelry: bartlettyarns

Bedhead Fiber
hello@bedheadfiber.com
bedheadfiber@gmail.com
Facebook: bedheadfiber
Instagram: bedheadfiber
Etsy: bedheadfiber

Cedar Hill Farm Company
1820 Duncan Rd.
Commerce, GA
(678) 468-7077
cedarhillyarns@gmail.com
www.cedarhillfarmcompany.com
Facebook: cerdarhillfarmcompany
Instagram: cerdarhillyarns
Twitter: cedarhillfarmco
Pinterest: Cedar Hill Farm Company

Eden Cottage Yarns
28 Ceres Rd.
Wetherby
West Yorkshire, United Kingdom
07961 263518
edencottageyarns@gmail.com
www.edencottageyarns.co.uk
Facebook: Eden-Cottage-Yarns
Instagram: EdenCottageYarns
Twitter: edencottage
Ravelry: vmagnus

Elemental Affects
17-555 Bubbling Wells Road
Desert Hot Springs, CA
(888) 699-2919
jeanedecoster@elementalaffects.com
www.elementalaffects.com
Instagram: elemental-affects
Ravelry: decostj

Hedgehog Fibres
8&9 Eastgate Way, Little Island
Cork, Ireland
+353 21 435 5808
contact@hedgehogfibres.com
www.hedgehogfibres.com
Facebook: Hedgehog-Fibres
Instagram: hedgehogfibres
Twitter: hedgehog_fibres
Ravelry: HedgehogFibres

Long Ridge Farm
116 Paine Rd
Westmoreland, NH
(603) 313-8398
longridgefarm@gmail.com
www.longridgefarm.com
Facebook: Long-Ridge-Farm
Twitter: umvarwanda
Ravelry: longridgefarm

Pik Ka Handbag
3110 1st Avenue South
Great Falls, MT
(406) 231-1314
pikkahandbag@outlook.com
www.pik-ka-handbag.com
Instagram: pik_ka_handbag

Pollinator Project
info@pollinator-project.om
www.pollinator-project.com
Instagram: pollinatorproject

Rosy Green Wool
Seitzstr. 19
80538 Munchen
Germany
info@rosygreenwool.com
www.rosygreenwool.com
Facebook: RosyGreenWool
Instagram: rosygreenwool
Ravelry: RosyGreenWool

The Woolen Rabbit
PO Box 1415
131 Pleasant St.
Conway, NH
(603) 447-5829
kim@thewoolenrabbit.com
www.thewoolenrabbit.com
Instagram: woolenrabbit
Ravelry: kim

Wandering Wool
9524 Watkins Rd.
Gaithersburg, MD
(202) 378-3040
wanderingwool@gmail.com
www.wanderingwool.com
Facebook: wanderingwool
Instagram: wanderingwool
Ravelry: WanderingWool

Photo Credits

pg. ii: Tasting Room. Source: Black Ankle Vineyards. n.d., Digital image.

pg. ii: Pedroncelli grapes. Source: Pedroncelli Winery. n.d., Digital image.

pg. ii: Sheep, horse. Source: Rosy Green Wool. n.d., Digital image.

pg. iii: Yarn pile. Source: Eden Cottage Yarns. n.d., Digital image.

pg. iii: Wine barrels. Source: Dry Creek Vineyards. n.d., Digital image.

pg. 10: Vines. Source: McGrail Vineyards and Winery. n.d., Digital image.

pg 10: Winery. Source: McGrail Vineyards and Winery. n.d., Digital image.

pg 10: Grapes. Source: McGrail Vineyards and Winery. n.d., Digital image.

pg 11: Winery. Source: McGrail Vineyards and Winery. n.d., Digital image.

pg. 13: Sheep face. Source: Bartlettyarns, Inc. n.d., Digital image.

pg. 15: Green yarn. Source: Bartlettyarns, Inc. n.d., Digital image.

pg. 15: Blue yarn on machine. Source: Bartlettyarns, Inc. n.d., Digital image.

pg. 17: Vineyard. Source: Black Ankle Vineyards. n.d., Digital image.

pg. 20: Vineyard. Source: Black Ankle Vineyards. n.d., Digital image.

pg. 20: Grapes. Source: Black Ankle Vineyards. n.d., Digital image.

pg. 21: Wine barrels. Source: Northleaf Winery. n.d., Digital image

pg. 21: Gradient yarns. Source: Wandering Wool. n.d., Digital image

pg. 26: Marker. Source: Northleaf Winery. n.d., Digital image.

pg. 26: Sign. Source: Northleaf Winery. n.d., Digital image.

pg. 28: Wine glasses. Source: Northleaf Winery. n.d., Digital image.

pg. 28: Winery beam. Source: Northleaf Winery. n.d., Digital image.

pg. 28: Christmas at Northleaf. Source: Northleaf Winery. n.d., Digital image

pg. 29: Sheep. Source: Rosy Green Wool. n.d., Digital image.

pg. 29: Winery. Source: Pedroncelli Winery. n.d., Digital image.

pg. 31: Organic Yarn. Source: Rosy Green Wool. n.d., Digital image.

pg. 34: Wine barrels. Source: Pedroncelli Winery. n.d., Digital image.

pg. 35: Cork. Source: Pedroncelli Winery. n.d., Digital image.

pg. 42: Vineyard. Source: Elk Cove Vineyard. n.d., Digital image.

pg. 45: Hands spinning wool. Source: Pi Ka Handbag. n.d., Digital image.

pg. 45: Sheep. Source: Pi Ka Handbag. n.d., Digital image.

pg. 45: Butte. Source: Colorado Cellars. n.d., Digital image.

pg. 50: Wine on table. Source: Colorado Cellars. n.d., Digital image.

pg. 51: Wine barrels. Source: Colorado Cellars. n.d., Digital image.

pg. 53: Yarn. Source: Cedar Hill Farm Company. n.d., Digital image.

pg. 53: Sheep. Source: Cedar Hill Farm Company. n.d., Digital image.

pg. 55: Sheep face. Source: Cedar Hill Farm Company. n.d., Digital image.

pg. 61: Dye Studio #1. Source: Hedgehog fibres. n.d., Digital image.

pg. 62: Dye Studio #2. Source: Hedgehog fibres. n.d., Digital image.

pg. 63: Dye Studio #3. Source: Hedgehog fibres. n.d., Digital image.

pg. 69: Sheep. Source: Elemental Affects. n.d., Digital image.

pg. 69: Wine rack. Source: Olalla Vineyard & Winery. n.d., Digital image.

pg. 74: Wine and candle. Source: Olalla Vineyards & Winery. n.d., Digital image.

pg. 75: Amphora. Source: Olalla Vineyard & Winery. n.d., Digital image.

pg. 75: Feet with grapes. Source: Olalla Vineyard & Winery. n.d., Digital image.

pg. 79: Spinning wheel. Source: The Woolen Rabbit. n.d., Digital image.

pg. 79: Spindle. Source: The Woolen Rabbit. n.d., Digital image.

pg. 82: Winery. Source: Dry Creek Vineyard. n.d., Digital image.

pg. 83: Winery interior. Source: Dry Creek Vineyard. n.d., Digital image.

pg. 86: Yarn. Source: Bedhead Fiber. n.d., Digital image.

pg. 90: Yarn and seeds. Source: Pollinator Project. n.d., Digital image.

pg. 91: Grape vines. Source: Breakwater Vineyards. n.d., Digital image.

pg. 93: Winery. Source: Breakwater Vineyards. n.d., Digital image.

pg. 92: Goat. Source: Breakwater Vineyards. n.d., Digital image.

pg. 93: Front porch. Source: Breakwater Vineyards. n.d., Digital image.

pg. 93: Winery interior . Source: Breakwater Vineyards. n.d., Digital image.

pg. 114: Table. Source: Olalla Vineyard & Winery. n.d., Digital image

Acknowledgements

This project would not have been possible without two extraordinary people. The first is my wife, Melissa, who has been a special part of my life since I first saw her across a classroom in the eigth grade, and whose hard work and dedication created most of the projects included in this book and drove the layout, editing and artistic direction. Second, my daughter Anna, who served as model, assistant photographer and whose many hours of dance lessons provided lots of time to write and think. Without your love and support, this would not have been possible – three is a magic number!

A special thank you for the support and contributions of those highlighted in this book. I hope that you are pleased with the results and that you all continue to enhance the beauty in the world through your vision and craft.

Here is to the artisans, dreamers and innovators – Cheers!

For more photos of the products featured in this book as well as "behind the scenes" images, visit Wool and Wine on our Facebook (woolandwinebook) and Instagram (woolandwinebook) pages! Questions and comments may be directed to woolandwinebook@gmail.com

85493162R00075

Made in the USA
Columbia, SC
20 December 2017